CW00971978

Books are to be return
the last date below.

707.823

2 7 . .. 2011

LIBREX-

QUESTIONS AND ANALYSIS IN HISTORY

Edited by Stephen J. Lee and Sean Lang

Other titles in this series:

THE COLD WAR

BRADLEY LIGHTBODY

ROUTLEDGE

London and New York

First published 1999 by Routledge
11 New Fetter Lane, London EC4P 4EE

Simultaneously published in the USA and Canada
by Routledge
29 West 35th Street, New York, NY 10001

Routledge is an imprint of the Taylor & Francis group

Typeset in Grotesque and Perpetua
by Keystroke, Jacaranda Lodge, Wolverhampton
Printed and bound in Great Britain by Clays Ltd, St Ives plc

British Library Cataloguing in Publication Data
A catalogue record for this book is available from the British Library

Library of Congress Cataloging in Publication Data
Lightbody, Bradley.
    The Cold War / Bradley Lightbody.
        p.   cm. – (Questions and analysis in history)
    Includes bibliographical references and index.
    ISBN 0–415–19526–8 (pbk)
    1. Cold War. I. Title. II. Series.
D843.L47   1999
909.82–dc 21   98-51997
                                              CIP

ISBN 0–415–19526–8

CONTENTS

SERIES PREFACE

Most history textbooks now aim to provide the student with interpretation, and many also cover the historiography of a topic. Some include a selection of sources.

So far, however, there have been few attempts to combine all the skills needed by the history student. Interpretation is usually found within an overall narrative framework and it is often difficult to separate out the two for essay purposes. Where sources are included, there is rarely much guidance as to how to answer the questions on them.

The Questions and Analysis series is therefore based on the belief that another approach should be added to those which already exist. It has two main aims.

The first is to separate narrative from interpretation so that the latter is no longer diluted by the former. Most chapters start with a background narrative section containing essential information. This material is then used in a section focusing on analysis through a specific question. The main purpose of this is to help to tighten up essay technique.

The second aim is to provide a comprehensive range of sources for each of the issues covered. The questions are of the type which appear on examination papers, and some have worked answers to demonstrate the techniques required.

The chapters may be approached in different ways. The background narratives can be read first to provide an overall perspective, followed by the analyses and then the sources. The alternative method is to work through all the components of each chapter before going on to the next.

ACKNOWLEDGEMENTS

Author and publisher are grateful to the following for permission to reproduce copyright material:

The *Guardian* ©, for an extract 12th September 1987; © Telegraph Group Limited London, for an extract 27th August 1991; *The Economist*, London for an extract 21st November 1987; *The Times* © and Times Newspapers Ltd 1962 for a sequence of extracts 22nd October 1962 to 28th October 1962 inclusive; Commager, Henry Steele, *Documents of American History, Vol. 11: Since 1898 ninth edition*, (Prentice-Hall, 1973); Bullock, Alan, *Hitler and Stalin: Parallel Lives* (HarperCollins, 1991); Eden, Sir Anthony, *The Full Circle: Memoirs of Sir Anthony Eden* (Cassell PLC, 1960); Volkogonov, Dmitri, *Stalin: Triumph and Tragedy* (Weidenfeld and Nicolson, 1991); Khrushchev, Nikita (trans. Strobe Talbott), *Khrushchev Remembers* (André Deutsch, 1971); Taylor, A.J.P., *The War Lords* (Hamish Hamilton, 1978); Dunbabin, J.P.D., *The Cold War: The Great Powers and Their Allies* (Longman, 1994: quotes reprinted by permission of Addison Wesley Longman Ltd); McCauley, Martin, *Origins of the Cold War, 1941–49* (Longman, 1983: quotes reprinted by permission of Addison Wesley Longman Ltd); Gaddis, John Lewis, *We Now Know*, (quotes reprinted by permission of Oxford University Press, 1997); Medvedev, Roy, *Khrushchev* (Blackwell, 1982); Yergin Daniel, *The Shattered Peace: The Origins of the Cold War and the National Security State* (André Deutsch, 1978: quotes reprinted by permission of the PetersFraser and Dunlop Group Ltd); Hutchinson for permission to quote from *Ronald Reagan: An American Life, the Autobiography*; and Cartermill International for permission to quote from Keesing's *Record of World Events* (Keesing's Worldwide, LLC).

INTRODUCTION

On 12th September 1990 the foreign secretaries of the four Allied powers who had occupied and divided Nazi Germany in 1945 met in Moscow and agreed to the reunification of Germany. The signatories were: Eduard Shevardnadze representing USSR; Roland Dumas representing France; Richard Cheney representing USA; and Douglas Hurd representing Great Britain. The foreign secretaries of divided Germany also signed their agreement: Hans-Dietrich Genscher representing the Federal Republic of Germany (West); Lothar de Maiziere representing the German Democratic Republic (East).

This agreement signalled the end of forty-five years of enmity that had divided the world and placed humanity under the shadow of the three-minute warning of nuclear destruction. The nuclear button was never depressed but millions did die in conventional wars around the world fought by proxy on behalf of the two superpowers.

The collapse of the Union of Soviet Socialist Republics (USSR) in 1991 finally ended the Cold War but it is more difficult to agree a starting point and this goes to the heart of the Cold War debate. To the West, the Cold War began on 5th March 1946, when Winston Churchill made his famous 'Iron Curtain' speech in Fulton, Missouri, and expressed in public British and American concerns about Soviet expansionism. To the East, the Cold War began in January 1918, when a hostile West intervened in the Russian Civil War and supported the White forces against the Bolshevik Red Army.

The disagreement as to whether communism or capitalism represented the main threat to world peace resulted in a rapidly escalating confrontation that divided the world into two armed camps and precipitated a series of well-documented flash points. Consequently this book avoids a conventional narrative of the Cold War but instead identifies the major questions and issues that mark the origins, escalation and the end of the Cold War. Each stage is examined through introductory narrative, document sources and in particular key questions and analysis of the major issues. If you are an A Level, Access or Degree History student, you will find this Question and Analysis approach invaluable to your preparation for assignments, seminars and examinations.

Finally, enjoy the challenge of the evidence and aim to arrive at judgements you can justify and defend.

Bradley Lightbody,
September 1998

1

EMERGENCE OF THE COLD WAR

BACKGROUND NARRATIVE

At 10.50 p.m. on 30th April 1945, the Red Army signalled the defeat of Nazi Germany by unfurling the Red Banner from the roof of the shattered Reichstag, Berlin. It was victory, but a victory overshadowed by the lack of agreement between the wartime Allies over the future of Europe.

The Red Army had advanced some 1500 miles from the gates of Moscow into the heart of Europe and this was of immediate concern to Great Britain and the United States. The Soviet Union, Great Britain and the United States were not natural allies but had been united by war against the common enemy: Nazi Germany. The pre-war relationship had been one of estrangement, given Western hostility to the Bolshevik Revolution of 1917 and a general fear of a revolutionary Marxist ideology that threatened world revolution.

The first wartime conference at Teheran in November 1943 was cordial and held out the prospect for future agreement but at the second conference, Yalta in February 1945, significant differences arose over the future of Poland and Germany. At this critical juncture in East–West relations President Roosevelt died, on 12th April 1945, and was succeeded by Vice-President Harry S Truman. Truman insisted that the Atlantic Charter signed by all of the nations at war with Germany must remain the basis of any post-war settlement. The Charter principles promised all nations a choice in their system of government as expressed in free and fair elections, but this conflicted with the Soviet Union's desire for 'friendly' governments in Eastern Europe.

The final conference of the war at Potsdam in July 1945, attempted to satisfy US and Soviet concerns but with mixed success. There was considerable mistrust on both sides and later each accused the other of breaking faith.

The non-co-operation between East and West was described as an 'Iron Curtain' by Churchill in a private telegram to Truman on 12th May 1945. These words later became the centrepiece of Churchill's famous speech of 5th March 1946, at Fulton, Missouri, when the failure to reach agreement was publicly acknowledged.

This speech was viewed in advance by President Truman, who thought it was admirable, whereas Stalin regarded it as harsh and confirmation of a threat to the Soviet Union. There were further attempts to break the deadlock in 1946–47 but in reality the Cold War had begun.

ANALYIS (1): TO WHAT EXTENT WAS THE COLD WAR INEVITABLE?

The orthodox and revisionist studies that dominated the early years of the Cold War blamed the Soviet Union and the United States respectively for attempting to impose their own political and economic ideologies upon Europe and the world. In both cases the Cold War was regarded as an inevitable clash between opposing ideologies as both the Soviet Union and the United States in 1945–47 attempted to impose a new world order based upon Marxism or capitalism.

The orthodox interpretation of the Soviet Union as a hostile, expansionist power dominated Western policy and thinking into the 1960s. American diplomats W. Averell Harriman and George F. Kennan in particular identified the Soviet Union as a threat to world peace to the extent that in April 1950 the National Security Agency asserted that the aim of the Soviet Union was nothing less than, 'absolute authority over the rest of the world'.[1]

This stark assessment of Soviet intentions dated back to 1917 and the Bolshevik Revolution. Lenin alarmed the West by endorsing the Marxist theory of inevitable conflict with capitalism until, 'ultimately one or the other must conquer'.[2] This threat of revolution cast a permanent shadow over pre-war relations, and the establishment of the Comintern to promote communism world-wide only served to heighten tension and opposition. The failure of the Western intervention in the Russian Civil War in 1918–20 and the subsequent survival of Bolshevism was greeted with dismay in the West and not least by Churchill who as British minister of war was one of the most trenchant opponents of communism. The Soviet Union was treated as a pariah nation not only because of the West's opposition to communist ideology but from moral opposition to 'red fascism', given the repressive nature of Lenin's and later Stalin's dictatorship.

After 1928, the transformation of the Soviet Union into an industrial and military power under Stalin's leadership only increased the sense of threat, and, if anything, the rise of Nazi Germany was welcomed as a 'bulwark against Bolshevism'. [3] The threat assessment was very much one of communism rather than fascism, despite Hitler's 'legal' revolution that supplanted Weimar democracy with a Nazi dictatorship and a foreign policy that openly addressed German expansion. The differences were that the Soviet Union's Marxist ideology challenged at an ideological level the concepts of liberalism and capitalism that formed the basis of Western society and government, and, at a more practical level, the fact that Lebensraum faced east. The evidence of Soviet hostility was more latent than actual but the Soviet involvement in the Spanish Civil War from 1936, the dismemberment of Poland in 1939 and the Soviet invasion of Finland in 1940 acted to confirm Stalin's hostile intent. The Kremlin watchers in the US Embassy in Riga, capital of Latvia, concluded that Stalin was biding his time looking for opportunities to exploit and was ultimately seeking world-wide communist revolution. By 1945, Stalin had annexed the Baltic States, pushed Poland's borders westwards and refused to withdraw from Eastern Europe until pro-Soviet governments were appointed rather than elected. Daniel Yergin identified the Soviet Union as a hostile, expansionist power in the 'Riga Axiom'[4] and it was here that the orthodox interpretation of the Cold War took firm root. Roosevelt was criticised for being too trusting in the face of this massive Soviet expansion. Feis argued that, rather than accept Soviet demands, it 'was better to risk a break with Stalin at Yalta'.[5]

At Potsdam it became an article of faith for Truman and Churchill that Stalin was using the dislocation of war to advance communism across Europe. Kennan, who was a diplomat in the US Embassy in Riga, expressed all of these fears in an uncompromising analysis, the 'Long Telegram' of February 1946, which identified the Bolsheviks as 'the last of that long succession of cruel and wasteful Russian rulers who have relentlessly forced their country on to ever new heights of military power'.[6] The subsequent Soviet rejection of the Baruch Plan to control nuclear weapons development also heightened Western concern about Soviet intentions.

In this context the Cold War was inevitable as the West had to oppose the Soviet Union for its own survival, but not everyone accepted the orthodox analysis of inevitable conflict. Looking through Soviet eyes, it was possible to regard Soviet actions as primarily defensive rather than expansionist. The US ambassador in Moscow in 1937–38, Joseph Davies, questioned the wisdom of the Riga Axiom, as did General Lucius Clay and the journalist Isaac Deutscher. The world revolutionary goals, espoused by Lenin and Trotsky, which so intimidated the West, had been abandoned by Stalin in 1928 in favour of 'socialism in one country'. The Comintern largely confined itself to propaganda and was eventually disbanded by Stalin in 1943 with no notable successes after twenty-five years of supposedly promoting revolution world-wide. Stalin regularly identified the West as a threat and in defending the high production targets of the first Five Year Plan in 1931 stated, 'either we do it or they crush us'.[7] Far from threatening the West, Stalin was intimidated by a hostile Nazi Germany and under the banner of collective security sought a defensive alliance with Britain and France. The rebuff of collective security and the Munich Agreement between Chamberlain and Hitler of 1938 convinced Stalin that Britain and France were 'encouraging the Germans to march East'.[8]

It was this fear that prompted Stalin to reach his own agreement with Hitler in the Nazi–Soviet Pact of 23rd August 1939 after years of what Stalin referred to as, 'pouring buckets of filth over each other's heads'.[9] The fact that Marxism and its antithesis fascism could come to an understanding for reasons of mutual gain indicated that ideology was no barrier to agreement.

After 1965 this evidence of a defensive Soviet Union coupled with shock at the scale and nature of the Vietnam War prompted a reassessment of American foreign policy in 1945–47. Paterson concluded that American policy 'assumed a communist monolith that did not exist'.[10]

The resulting revisionist interpretation of the Cold War identified the Atlantic Charter of 1941 as an attempt at a Pax Americana that made the Cold War inevitable. Instead of Stalin being expansionist and hostile, he was merely defending the Soviet Union against US policies that were designed to undermine communism. The Atlantic Charter principles carried forward the 1918 Wilsonian aims of a democratic world and 'open-door' economics, but such liberal principles were alien to the Soviet system of government and made disagreement inevitable.

Both Great Britain and the Soviet Union ended the war virtually bankrupt, but the United States' GNP had more than doubled and placed that country in a commanding position, giving rise to the suspicion that the commitment to open-door economics was an attempt to open up the British Empire and the whole of Europe to American economic penetration. The Conservative MP Robert Boothby complained in the House of Commons that the United States' aim was to 'open the markets of the world for the benefit of the United States of America'.[11] This suspicion was supported by the liberal conditions attached to Lend–Lease payments and the establishment of the World Bank and the IMF at Bretton Woods in 1944, all of which favoured US trade.

The later US suspension of Lend–Lease payments to the Soviet Union and the reluctance to endorse reparations to compensate the Soviet Union for the cost of the war were equally interpreted as attempts at economic blackmail. Finally, at Potsdam the US nuclear monopoly was used by Truman as a trump card to try to force Soviet compliance with the Atlantic Charter but the result was only to increase division and make the Cold War inevitable. The later rearming of West Germany and admittance to NATO in May 1949 were equally offensive to the Soviet Union after the losses of the Second World War, and deepened the Cold War hostility.

The revisionist argument of inevitable conflict is contradicted by Roosevelt's pragmatic and openly flexible approach at Teheran in 1943 and Yalta in 1945. Roosevelt was willing to concede Soviet spheres of influence if it meant winning Soviet co-operation within the United Nations and a partnership to police the world. He was an idealist committed to liberalism, but he recognised the reality of Soviet power and hoped that over a period of ten to twenty years sufficient trust would be established to permit the relaxation of the Soviet dictatorship. Later, in 1946, US Secretaries James Byrnes and Henry Wallace attempted to maintain Roosevelt's pragmatism but failed against an administration convinced of the Riga Axiom.

The inconsistencies in the orthodox and revisionist interpretations of the Cold War were exposed, after 1972, by John Lewis Gaddis, in particular, in a succession of books that collectively ushered in the post-revisionist interpretation. The Cold War was judged to be a product of the misjudgements of both the United States and the Soviet Union during the wartime negotiations rather than an inevitable conflict. Stalin had misjudged the nature of Western democracy and the restrictions it placed upon Churchill and Roosevelt to strike deals, whereas Truman and Churchill had misjudged Stalin's sense of insecurity and need for financial assistance to restore the Soviet Union.

The death of Roosevelt on 12th April 1945 removed the person most able to bridge the divide and broker agreement.

In addition, public opinion in 1945 recognised the sacrifice of the Soviet Union and found any idea of future conflict difficult to accept. The day after Churchill's 'Iron Curtain' speech the *Chicago Sun* commented: 'Let Mr Truman's rejection of the poisonous doctrines declared by Mr Churchill be prompt and emphatic.'[12] Likewise, British newspapers were so positive towards the Soviet Union that 'the Foreign Office worked assiduously behind the scenes to correct the pro-Soviet stance by editors'.[13]

The even-handed nature of the post-revisionist interpretation is currently under threat from the 'new' Cold War research. The collapse of the Soviet Union in 1991 has opened up Soviet archives and permitted Soviet writers to express their views openly. The leading post-revisionist historian John Lewis Gaddis has examined Soviet archives and reached the new conclusion that the Cold War was the product of 'authoritarianism in general and Stalin in particular'.[14] The focus has returned to the orthodox interpretation and Stalin but this does not entirely end the debate. Russian writers Zubok and Pleshakov, while accepting Stalin's responsibility, add that 'there was no master plan in the Kremlin' and 'they [Russians] were not the only culprits in the conflict'.[15]

In conclusion, the ruthless totalitarian nature of the Soviet occupation of Eastern Europe made the division of Europe inevitable but not a global Cold War.

Questions

1. Why did the Riga Axiom dominate Western policy?
2. How far did the Atlantic Charter represent a Pax Americana?

ANALYSIS (2): WHY WERE THE WARTIME ALLIES UNABLE TO REACH AGREEMENT IN 1945?

The wartime Allies were unable to reach agreement in 1945 primarily due to the inability of the Soviet Union and the United States to square the circle of the Soviet domination of Eastern Europe against the American and British commitment to democracy and free trade. Both the Soviet Union and the United States failed sufficiently to acknowledge and accommodate each other's vital interests and in the absence of compromise agreement became impossible.

The wartime alliance of 1942–45 was unexpected. It was a product of Hitler's decision to declare war upon the Soviet Union and the United States in 1941 while still at war with Great Britain. The common bond of comrades in arms united Churchill, Roosevelt and Stalin but beyond this there was little agreement and in particular the existence of two very different world views was never reconciled.

Churchill and Roosevelt presented the democratic world view in the Atlantic Charter of 14th August 1941 when they agreed eight guiding principles to govern the post-war world. On 1st January 1942 the Charter principles were all incorporated into the Declaration of the United Nations that was signed by all of the nations at war with Germany. A.J.P. Taylor regarded Roosevelt as 'a man of ideals'[16] and the principles all reflected his vision of a world community of democratic nations committed to free trade and policed by the United Nations. However, within a Marxist world view the principles all represented the advance of capitalism rather than a value-free, neutral statement of common aims. According to Volkogonov, Stalin simply 'pushed ideological antagonism out of sight' for pragmatic reasons.[17]

There was no certainty of victory in 1942 and the Soviet Union desperately needed US Lend–Lease assistance and the opening of a second front to ensure its survival. Consequently, the Declaration placed the Allies on a collision course and in 1945 Poland proved to be the point of impact when Truman and Stalin clashed over the democratic credentials of the new Polish government.

On 12th August 1942 Churchill travelled to Moscow with news of delays to the establishment of the second front. Deutscher described this meeting as 'acrimonious and stormy'.[18] While Churchill was defending the Allied position the Soviet Army was defending Stalingrad and enduring heavy casualties in one of the most significant battles of the war. Approximately 800,000 Soviet soldiers and civilians were killed in this single conflict compared to 375,000 British and 405,000 American casualties for the *entire* war. Estimates of the total Soviet casualties for the war vary, but Lee calculates a minimum of 23 million.[19] In Deutscher's view, Stalin was suspicious that the Allies were content to watch the Soviet and Nazi armies destroy each other on the battlefield and rid Europe of both fascism and communism.[20] This suspicion was compounded in May 1943 when the second front was further postponed in favour of Allied landings in Sicily and Italy. Khrushchev, in his memoirs, confirmed this suspicion and stated that the intention of the Allies was to 'bleed us dry', and then at the end of the war to 'dictate their will to us'.[21] Volkogonov identified Stalin's decision to disband the Comintern and his denial that the Soviet Union wished to 'Bolshevise' other states as evidence of his concern.[22]

Roosevelt was alert to Stalin's suspicions and at the first wartime conference in Teheran in November 1943 he struck up a warm accord with Stalin, even to the extent of calling him 'Uncle Joe'. Teheran ended on a positive note with broad agreements over the future of Poland and Germany and confirmation of the timing of the second front. It seemed that agreement was possible.

By the second wartime conference at Yalta in February 1945 it was a very different war. The Russians had entered Germany only 100 miles from Berlin and the Allies were on the Rhine at Nijmegen. Victory was certain, and in these circumstances the differences between the 'Big Three' soon began to emerge. Churchill was anxious to re-establish British Empire interests in the Balkans and the Pacific and Stalin was insistent upon pro-Soviet governments in Eastern Europe. Both contradicted the United Nations Declaration, which Roosevelt was anxious to preserve as much as possible. Stalin had once remarked to the British foreign secretary Anthony Eden in 1941 that he regarded declarations as 'algebra' but agreements as 'practical arithmetic' and he much preferred practical arithmetic. In McCauley's assessment Yalta was 'pure algebra' to Stalin.[23] The warning was clear to those who listened. Stalin's practical arithmetic was the Red Army occupation of Eastern Europe, the 23 million Soviet war dead and the estimated cost of $20 billion to rebuild the shattered Soviet Union. Stalin was seeking confirmation of a Soviet sphere of interest along with practical financial support either from the Allies or in reparations from a defeated Germany. Roosevelt was willing to be pragmatic to carry the wartime alliance forward into peacetime but he had to satisfy American public opinion and Congress. Stalin had no constituency to please and underestimated the importance of Western public opinion. His attitude to Poland in particular made agreement very difficult for Great Britain and the United States. Great Britain had gone to war in 1939 to defend Polish democracy, and to replace a Nazi dictatorship with a Soviet dictatorship was difficult for Western public opinion to accept.

Despite these differences, Yalta ended with apparent success, mainly due to the determination of Roosevelt to reach an agreement. He conceded the need for reparations and, as Martin Gilbert comments, 'to Churchill's surprise' Stalin promised to hold 'free' elections in Poland.[24] In addition Stalin agreed to participate in the United Nations and offered the United States assistance in the continuing war against Japan.

Only three weeks after Yalta relationships were soured when Stalin ordered the arrest and deportation to labour camps of thousands of Polish intellectuals and democrats and accused the United States and Great Britain of preparing a separate peace with the Nazi High Command. Roosevelt expressed his concerns to Stalin and resolutely defended the Allied position but his death came just as the first serious rifts in the alliance had emerged. Without the rapid restoration of mutual trust, the alliance was in danger of collapse.

The new president of the United States, Harry Truman, met with his advisers on 20th April 1945, but trust was not on the agenda. McCauley ascribes the change in policy to hard-liners like Harriman, the US ambassador to the Soviet Union, who expressed the view that the Russians were 'barbarians' whose advance into the heart of Europe had to be resisted.[25] The judgement of Soviet actions was that Stalin was moving beyond legitimate security needs into an expansion of Soviet territory driven by the revolutionary Marxist aim of world domination. Truman accepted a brief to hold Stalin to the Declaration of Liberated Europe and to respect democracy.

This shift in American thinking was immediately obvious on 23rd April 1945, when Truman met with the Soviet Union's foreign minister, Vyacheslav Molotov, and abruptly told him to respect the Yalta agreement. Instead of mutual trust being restored, there was only mutual anger. McCauley records that Molotov went 'white' with rage and objected to how he had been received.[26]

This was followed by the cancellation of further US Lend–Lease assistance to the Soviet Union on 11th May 1945, implemented so abruptly that ships already at sea were ordered to return to port. Shipments were later restored, but the point had been made. There was a different president in the White House and a different policy.

Stalin had misjudged the West's commitment to democracy and rejected a compromise over Poland that would have allowed the communist 'Lublin' Poles and the democratic 'London Poles' to form a strictly neutral government, like the Government of Finland. The application of the 'Finland model' to the whole of Eastern Europe may have satisfied Stalin's security concerns and the Western fear of an expansion of communism. The opportunity for agreement was lost as Stalin saw no need to negotiate over territory that had been liberated at huge cost to the Red Army and because he believed that Roosevelt had conceded a Soviet sphere of influence at Yalta. Stalin was also aware that free elections would probably result in the rejection of communism and consequently he rejected the West's demand for democracy.

A cool atmosphere of charge and counter-charge set a tone of confrontation for Potsdam and the last conference of the war. Truman delayed the start of the Potsdam Conference to 17th July 1945, in the knowledge that Operation Trinity – the test explosion of the world's first atomic bomb – was scheduled for 16th July 1945, in the Alamogordo Desert, New Mexico. The development of nuclear weapons had not been shared with the Soviet Union and there was an expectation that the demonstration of the bomb would encourage Stalin to be more compliant. Churchill, according to Gilbert, wanted the United States to use the bomb to 'restrain the Russians'.[27]

Churchill lost his seat at the conference on 26th July 1945 when he was defeated in the British general election and was replaced by Clement Attlee, the new Labour prime minister. This, however, was somewhat irrelevant as the two power brokers were the Soviet Union and the United States. Churchill's observation at Yalta that power was slipping away from Great Britain was proved to be correct. The talks were polite but combative and Stalin made it clear that the Soviet Union would decide what was going to happen in Eastern Europe. Agreement depended upon mutual compromise.

It was in Truman's gift to satisfy Soviet security concerns by recognising a Soviet sphere of influence in Eastern Europe and to offer financial assistance to rebuild the Soviet Union. It was in Stalin's gift to ease US fears of communist expansion by granting more autonomy and freedom to the governments of Eastern Europe. There were no compromises and opinions on both sides remained firmly entrenched. On the surface Potsdam was a success but both sides knew that deep unresolved differences remained, especially over the future of Germany and reparations.

Inside the five months from Yalta to Potsdam in 1945 the Cold War emerged from the polarised demands of the Soviet Union for security and the United States for liberty.

Questions

1. To what extent were the Soviet demands over Eastern Europe justifiable?
2. How significant to the progress of the wartime negotiations was the death of Roosevelt?

SOURCES

The first set of sources deals with the clash of aims and interests between Russia and the West and the second set the issue of mutual mistrust which arose over Poland in particular.

1. AIMS AND INTERESTS

Source A: extract from Churchill's 'Iron Curtain' speech, 5th March 1946, Fulton, Missouri.

Winston Churchill, on a speaking tour of the United States, publicly declared his opposition to the occupation of Eastern Europe by the Soviet Union.

From Stettin in the Baltic to Trieste in the Adriatic, an Iron Curtain has descended across the continent. Behind that line lie all the capitals of the ancient states of Central and Eastern Europe – Warsaw, Berlin, Prague, Vienna, Budapest, Belgrade, Bucharest and Sofia. All these famous cities and the populations around them lie in the Soviet sphere, and all are subject in one form or another, not only to Soviet influence, but to a very high and increasing measure of control from Moscow.

Athens alone with its immortal glories is free to decide its future at an election under British, American and French observation. The Russian-dominated Polish government has been encouraged to make enormous and wrongful inroads upon Germany and mass expulsions of millions of Germans on a scale grievous and undreamed of are now taking place. The communist parties which were very small in all these Eastern states of Europe have been raised to pre-eminence and power far beyond their numbers and are seeking everywhere to obtain totalitarian control.

Source B: extract from Stalin's reply to Churchill, 13th March 1946.

Stalin speaking in defence of the occupation of Eastern Europe by the Soviet Union in *Pravda*.

The following circumstances should not be forgotten. The Germans made their invasion of the USSR through Finland, Poland, Romania, Bulgaria and Hungary. The Germans were able to make their invasion through these countries because at the time governments hostile to the Soviet Union existed in these countries . . . Possibly in some quarters an inclination is felt to forget about these colossal sacrifices of the Soviet people which secured the liberation of Europe from the Hitlerite yoke. But the Soviet Union cannot forget about them. And so what can there be surprising about the fact that the Soviet Union, anxious for its future safety, is trying to see to it that governments loyal in their attitude to the Soviet Union should exist in these countries? How can anyone who has not taken leave of his senses describe these peaceful aspirations of the Soviet Union as expansionist tendencies on the part of our state?

Source C: a barbarian invasion.

US State Department papers recorded the opinions of Ambassador Harriman, 20th April 1945.

Ambassador Harriman said that in effect what we were faced with was a 'barbarian invasion of Europe', that Soviet control over any foreign country did not merely mean influence on their foreign relations but the extension of the Soviet system with secret police, extinction of freedom of speech, etc.

Source D: extract from the Atlantic Charter, 14th August 1941.

The Atlantic Charter was agreed between Churchill and Roosevelt onboard the battleship *Prince of Wales* cruising off the Newfoundland coast, 9th–12th August 1941. Here, for brevity, the first four of the eight principles are reproduced.

Joint declaration of the President of the United States of America and the Prime Minister, Mr Churchill, representing His Majesty's Government in the United Kingdom, being met together, deem it right to make known certain common principles in the national policies of their respective countries on which they base their hopes for a better future for the world.

First, their countries seek no aggrandizement, territorial or other;
Second, they desire to see no territorial changes that do not accord with the freely expressed wishes of the peoples concerned;
Third, they respect the right of all peoples to choose the form of government under which they will live; and they wish to see sovereign rights and self-government restored to those who have been forcibly deprived of them;
Fourth, they will endeavour with due respect for their existing obligations to further the enjoyment by all states, great or small, victor or vanquished, of access, on equal terms, to the trade and to the raw materials of the world which are needed for their economic prosperity . . .

Questions

*1. Explain what Churchill meant by an 'Iron Curtain' in Source A.
2. In what ways do Stalin (Source B) and Harriman (Source C) differ in their attitudes to Eastern Europe?
3. In what ways do the concerns of Churchill (Source A) and the Atlantic Charter principles (Source D) conflict with Stalin's opinions (Source B)?

4. Using your own knowledge and with reference to all of the sources, answer the following question: To what extent did the Soviet quest for security in Eastern Europe against the American quest for liberty make the Cold War inevitable?

Worked answer

*1. [Source questions often start with an opening question worth only 1 or 2 marks which demands a definition of a word or term in the context of the source. The answer should be direct and to the point. A one sentence answer is all that is required.]

In line one of Source A the term 'Iron Curtain' is a vivid piece of imagery used by Churchill to describe the impenetrable border that divided Soviet-occupied Eastern Europe from the rest of Europe.

SOURCES

2. MUTUAL MISTRUST

Source E: extract from Kennan's 'Long Telegram', 22nd February 1946.

George Kennan was an American diplomat partly responsible for the formulation of the 'Riga Axiom' and credited with influencing President Truman and the course of American foreign policy through the views expressed in his 'Long Telegram'.

It was no coincidence that Marxism, which had smouldered ineffectively for half a century in Western Europe, caught hold and blazed for the first time in Russia. Only in this land which had never known a friendly neighbour or indeed any tolerant equilibrium of separate powers, either internal or international, could a doctrine thrive which viewed economic conflicts of society as insoluble by peaceful means. After establishment of Bolshevik regime, Marxist dogma, rendered even more truculent and intolerant by Lenin's interpretation, became a perfect vehicle for sense of insecurity with which Bolsheviks, even more than previous Russian rulers, were afflicted. In this dogma, with its basic altruism of purpose, they found justification for their instinctive fear of outside world, for the dictatorship without which they did not know how to rule, for cruelties they did not dare not to inflict, for sacrifices they felt bound to demand. In the name of Marxism they sacrificed every single ethical value in their methods and tactics.

Source F: Soviet wartime suspicions.

Khrushchev recorded Soviet suspicions of the Allies in his memoirs.

It's difficult to judge what the intentions of the Allies were towards the end of the war. I wouldn't exclude the possibility that they desired to put a still greater burden on the shoulders of the Soviet Union and to bleed us even more. Or perhaps it's as they explained: they weren't sufficiently prepared for a landing. Their arms production wasn't sufficiently developed. They needed more time, and so on. Both explanations were probably true but I think they were mostly dictated by their desire to bleed us dry so that they could come in at the last stages and determine the fate of the world. They wanted to take advantage of the results of the war and impose their will not only on their enemy, Germany, but on their ally, the USSR, as well.

Source G: extract from Stalin's statement on Poland at Yalta, February 1945.

The future of Poland was an issue that divided Stalin and Churchill in particular at Yalta but one on which Roosevelt was prepared to compromise. Stalin insisted upon a pro-Soviet government whereas Churchill upheld the right of the pre-war democratic government of Poland, the 'London Poles', to return to Poland.

It is a question of honour because the Russians have committed many sins against the Poles in the past, and the Soviet government wishes to make amends. And it is a question of security because Poland presents the gravest of strategic problems for the Soviet Union. Throughout history, Poland has served as a corridor for enemies coming to attack Russia. Why have these enemies found it so easy up to this time to pass through Poland? Mainly because Poland was weak. The Polish corridor could not be closed from outside solely by Russian force. It could only be reliably closed from inside by Poland's own efforts. That meant Poland had to be strong. That is why the Soviet Union is interested in the creation of a mighty, free and independent Poland. The Polish question is a question of life and death for the Soviet state.

Source H: Churchill at Potsdam.

Churchill expressed his concern about the future of Poland at the Potsdam Conference, July 1945.

We agree the Polish question should be discussed, including the winding up of the London government. We hope the Marshal and the President will recognise that England was made the home of the Polish government which fought against the Axis. England has the burden of winding up these obligations.

Questions

1. Explain what is meant by the phrase 'insoluble by peaceful means' as it appears in Source E.
*2. How far do Sources E and F provide evidence of mutual mistrust?
3. How important was the issue of Poland to Stalin (Source G) and Churchill (Source H)?
4. Using your wider knowledge and the evidence of all of the sources, answer the following question: Why did the wartime Allies fail to reach agreement over the future of Europe?

Worked answer

*2. Sources E and F both demonstrate a high level of American and Soviet mutual mistrust. In Source E Kennan provides an extremely negative assessment of a Russia 'which had never known a friendly neighbour', which adopted a hostile Marxist policy, established a 'dictatorship' that inflicted 'cruelties' and 'sacrificed every single ethical value'. The overall impression is to rule out any question of trust. In Source F Khrushchev provides a very direct statement of a lack of trust in the Allies when he questioned their motives in delaying the second front. Khrushchev was suspicious that the Allies were deliberately leaving the Soviet Union to shoulder the burden of the war with the intention 'to bleed us dry' and after the war to 'impose their will . . . on . . . the USSR'.

2

CONFRONTATION

In 1947 the American journalist Walter Lippmann, writing in the *New York Herald Tribune*, popularised the term 'Cold War' to describe the mounting hostility between East and West.

President Truman, with a less popular touch but perhaps more accuracy, preferred the term 'War of Nerves' to describe the tense uncertainty that surrounded Soviet intentions in the post-war world. In February 1946 Stalin had announced a build-up of Soviet heavy industry in a speech that appeared to threaten the West. Truman sought an explanation of Soviet behaviour and George Kennan in Moscow sent the 5540-word cable to Washington known as the 'Long Telegram', with the opinion that the Soviet Union was an expansionist, hostile power. Kennan's assessment was swiftly endorsed by Churchill in his 'Iron Curtain' speech of March 1946, followed by the State Department's Clifford Report in September 1946.

On 12th March 1947, following a potential Soviet threat to Greece and Turkey, Truman announced the Truman Doctrine and committed the United States to the defence of the free world against totalitarian dictatorships. The Soviet Union was not directly mentioned but it was clear to all that Truman had decided to confront the Soviet Union in a policy Kennan later dubbed 'Containment'. On 5th June 1947 the announcement of the Marshall Plan promised generous financial aid to assist in the recovery of Europe but the Soviet Union declined to participate. The result was confrontation as the West faced the Sovietisation of Eastern Europe that had occurred in 1945–47, the Berlin Crisis of

1948, the establishment of Communist China in 1949 and finally the Korean War of 1950–53.

The death of Stalin on 5th March 1953 ended the 'War of Nerves' as the new Soviet leadership relaxed the worst excesses of Stalin's dictatorship and sought a new understanding and agreement with the West through 'peaceful coexistence'.

ANALYSIS (1): HOW FAR DID STALIN THREATEN WORLD PEACE?

At the end of the Second World War the Red Army dwarfed Allied forces and it was in immediate striking range of the Balkans, Middle East and Far East. Stalin failed to make his goals explicit and this created considerable doubt and uncertainty about Soviet intentions. The result was the assumption of a threat to world peace but ultimately Stalin's threat was more psychological than actual.

The Soviet Union ended the war militarily triumphant but economically ruined. The whole of western Russia was a wasteland of destruction with an estimated 25 million homeless people in search of food, clothing and shelter. Famine was widespread with reports of 'people eating dead animals and the bark of fallen trees . . . of a peasant woman and her sons murdering her small daughter and eating her dead body'.[1] In addition, as late as 1954, the Soviet Union faced disruption by roving bands of anti-communist partisans. To restore the economy, 'men were needed in the factories and on farms'[2] and consequently in May 1945 Stalin demobilised the Red Army, which decreased in Soviet estimations from 11,365,000 to 2,874,000 soldiers.

The Pentagon acknowledged the weakness of the Soviet Union and in May 1945 regarded a future war as more likely from a resurgent Japan or Germany than 'a defensive and technologically backward Soviet Union'.[3] The United States initially discounted any Soviet threat, insulated from the Soviet Union by two oceans and optimistic that the post-war meetings of foreign ministers, in London from September to October 1945, would finalise the Potsdam discussions and produce a settlement.

There was no similar optimism in the Soviet Union as Stalin was personally convinced that the West was determined to destroy the Soviet Union. According to Zubok and Pleshakov, the US nuclear monopoly 'threw the Kremlin leader off balance' and resulted in an obsession with security against a surprise attack from the West.[4]

Khrushchev confirmed this, noting that Stalin placed 'anti-aircraft units around Moscow on a twenty-four-hour alert'.[5] As a further measure of his paranoia, Stalin ruthlessly screened all returning Soviet POWs in NKVD camps for any trace of Western influences or sympathies that might question the Soviet system. The Soviet Union had been caught off guard in 1941 but security was now the watchword and Fortress Russia was the order of the day. According to Bullock, Stalin's 'primary aim can be summed up as security after the traumatic experience of the war'.[6]

Consequently, Stalin was determined to tighten rather than relax the Sovietisation of Eastern Europe to create a buffer zone against any renewal of Western hostility. At the London Conference of Foreign Ministers, Soviet intransigence led to a repeat of the Potsdam stalemate and it became obvious that Stalin expected the West to accept separate spheres of influence in Europe. He justified Soviet actions in Eastern Europe as a matter of national security as the pre-war governments had been avowedly anti-communist, with Romania and Hungary in particular directly assisting the Nazi invasion of the Soviet Union. The Western concern for democracy struck Stalin as a double standard, as all of the pre-war governments, except for Czechoslovakia, had been dictatorships. Similarly, the West had at first tolerated and to some extent welcomed the fascist dictatorships of Mussolini, Hitler and Franco. Stalin also noted the determination of Britain and France to re-establish their empires around the world in defiance of national liberation movements, with France in particular waging war in Indochina without Western protest.

Stalin, looking at a map of the Soviet conquests in 1944, remarked to Molotov that there was too much red and the West was bound to oppose Soviet gains. His prophecy was correct, as both Churchill and Truman refused to dilute their commitment to democracy and rejected any agreement based on separate spheres of influence. It was here that a possible opportunity for settlement was missed. Stalin 'did not want confrontation with his former allies but he did not know how to avoid it'.[7] When Stalin pressed the Soviet claim to northern Iran and the Black Sea Straits, it appeared to confirm a Soviet threat to the wider world.

Stalin's interest in Iran was border security in general and oil in particular. A supply of oil was vital to the recovery of the Soviet economy, but although Iran granted oil concessions to Britain, similar oil concessions were denied to the Soviet Union. Stalin ignored a deadline for the withdrawal of the Red Army from Iran but it was a measure of Soviet weakness that the Soviet Union finally bowed to

Western pressure and complied. To the West, the threat of Soviet expansionism had been checked, but to Stalin the denial of oil supplies along with the ending of Lend–Lease, the rejection of reparations and the refusal to share nuclear technology added up to a Western strategy to weaken the Soviet Union.

Truman also opposed the Soviet claim to the Black Sea Straits as, 'an open bid to obtain control over Turkey'.[8] However, the straits were the main gateway for Soviet trade, and control of them had long been a goal of Tsarist foreign policy rather than a sudden burst of Soviet expansionism. At Teheran in 1942 Churchill had conceded that major revision of the straits was necessary, but in response to Turkish protests in 1946 a permanent US fleet was deployed to the Mediterranean to underline opposition to any change.

Stalin viewed the West as unremittingly hostile and this was the theme of his traditional eve of election address to the Supreme Soviet on 9th February 1946. Stalin was back in siege mode as he had been in the 1930s and he warned of a future capitalist war and the need for the Soviet Union to implement three Five Year Plans to rebuild and extend Soviet heavy industry. In comments reminiscent of 1931 Stalin urged the Soviet people to maximum effort and insisted, 'it can be done and we must do it'.[9] Kennan, in Moscow, reported the speech as a threat of war rather than simply a possibility of war, and 'Washington was stunned . . . Justice William O'Douglas called it the declaration of World War Three.'[10] Truman's administration was convinced of a Soviet threat yet Stalin's speech contained no direct threat and, if anything, was vague and ambiguous. There were no Soviet equivalents to Truman's 'iron fist', Churchill's 'we will raze their cities', or the United States' representative at the United Nations John Foster Dulles's 'massive retaliation'.

The decisive break with the Soviet Union occurred on 12th March 1947, when Truman announced the Truman Doctrine to defend Greece and Turkey against 'totalitarianism' but no one was in any doubt that he meant communism. Truman was convinced that Stalin was assisting the Greek communist partisans but in reality there was 'no evidence of Soviet involvement in the Greek civil war'.[11] On this basis Truman committed the United States to the global defence of freedom and ignored the dictatorial record of the governments of Greece and Turkey that Mooney and Brown described as 'fully fledged squalid little dictatorships in their own right'.[12] Truman's open-ended commitment to any nation was challenged by Kennan, who was increasingly critical of the combative tone of US policy and later regretted 'his own hyperbole', and role in identifying the Soviet Union as a threat.[13] The subsequent Marshall Plan initiated in June 1947 was more in keeping with Kennan's preferred approach, but after the declaration of the Truman Doctrine, 'Stalin saw the whole thing as a trap, and refused to participate'.[14]

The economic revival of Europe and in particular the liberal attitude towards defeated Germany and Japan alarmed Stalin and he predicted 'a capitalist coalition . . . would be ready for war in five to six years'.[15] Stalin looked to Fortress Russia and created the Cominform in September 1947, brutally enforced Soviet rule in Eastern Europe in 1947–49 and challenged the West in Berlin in June 1948. In each case Stalin acted to control more tightly and secure the new Soviet border in Europe but his aggression and unilateral decisions increased the sense of threat in the West. The British Foreign Office was in no doubt about the nature of Stalin's threat and declared that the Soviet aim was 'the establishment of a world dictatorship'.[16] However, Stalin's hostility towards Tito and ambivalent attitude to the French and Italian communist parties indicated that Stalin placed personal power above communist expansion.

Stalin's actions ultimately acted against him as they silenced the pragmatists in the American and British governments and wider media and panicked Western Europe into reviewing its own security. The result was the formation of NATO in April 1949. It is noticeable that the Soviet Union only countered with the Warsaw Pact in May 1954, approximately one week after Germany was admitted to NATO. The fear of German rearmament and a capitalist coalition was all too real in the Soviet Union.

The detonation of a Soviet atomic bomb on 14th July 1949 ended the United States' nuclear monopoly and created war fever. Senator McMahon declared 'blow them off the face of the Earth . . . we haven't much time,'[17] despite the fact that the Soviet Union had no delivery system capable of reaching the United States.

American nerves were further unsettled on 1st October 1949 by Mao Zedong's declaration of Communist China, which *Time* magazine greeted as 'the red tide that threatens to engulf the world'.[18] The West saw a communist monolith but Stalin saw a rival power and a possible threat to the Soviet Union's national interests in the Far East. There was no communist solidarity and Mao complained that winning concessions from Stalin was like 'pulling teeth'.[19]

The National Security Council (NSC), in a new assessment of the Soviet threat in April 1950, declared, 'the survival of the world is at stake'.[20] This grim judgement appeared to be confirmed in April 1950 with the outbreak of the Korean War. Truman feared 'World War

Three'[21] but the war was 'not Stalin's brainchild'[22] and only had his limited support. Stalin had allowed himself to be convinced by Kim Il Sung that the North could achieve a swift victory over the South aided by a popular rising of South Korean workers. The rising never happened and Stalin subsequently distanced the Soviet Union from the war and refused to permit direct Soviet military assistance, although he did cynically encourage China to intervene in an attempt to salvage some credibility from what was a colossal misjudgement. This, more than any other event, convinced the world that Stalin was a threat to world peace, but essentially it was the continuation of the Korean civil war.

Stalin finally died from a stroke at 9.50 a.m. on 5th March 1953, not plotting and planning a global revolution but a further purge of the Party and a group of Jewish doctors who were the latest in a long line of enemies to be denounced. As always, Stalin's threat was more internal than external. By the end of the dictator's life, Volkogonov estimated that 'Stalin's victims amounted to between 19.52 and 22 million',[23] all in an unceasing quest for blind obedience.

Khrushchev, in delivering his denunciation of Stalin at the Twentieth Congress of the Soviet Communist Party in February 1956, utterly condemned Stalin's style of government and blamed him for 'many gross mistakes in his direction of the Soviet Union's foreign policy'.[24] Stalin rarely sought the opinions of his Politburo but tended to act on instinct, and he forced those around him to engage in a deadly dance of survival to predict correctly and endorse his policies.

Ultimately, Stalin's threat to the world was more shadow than substance, but the shadow alone transfixed the West and resulted in unbridled confrontation.

Questions

1. How far did Stalin's demands reflect the security needs of the Soviet Union?
2. To what extent was Stalin's threat more internal than external?

ANALYSIS (2): WHY DID THE UNITED STATES' POLICY OF CO-OPERATION WITH THE SOVIET UNION TRANSFORM TO CONFRONTATION?

The United States had high ideals for the post-war world, and, having defeated Nazi and Japanese totalitarianism, felt betrayed by the extension of Soviet totalitarianism. The West as a whole had deep anxiety about Soviet intentions and at first the response was one of 'containment', but when the Cold War turned hot in Korea in 1950, the United States entered into world-wide military confrontation.

In the immediate post-war period American attitudes towards the Soviet Union were highly positive. *Life* magazine regularly published favourable accounts of Stalin and the Soviet Union to the extent that the NKVD was described as 'a national police similar to the FBI'.[25] However, the extension of Soviet totalitarianism to Eastern Europe soon dispelled such cosy notions and the United States was forced to come to terms with a de facto Soviet sphere of interest that was in open breach of Yalta commitments to free elections. To maintain co-operation would mean recognising the Soviet sphere and abandoning the people of Eastern Europe to communism. George Kennan proposed such a policy in March 1945 but State Department official Charles Bohlen dismissed the idea, stating, 'foreign policy of that kind cannot be made in a democracy'.[26] This refusal to accept the Soviet domination of Eastern Europe prevented any meaningful agreement at the London Conference of Foreign Ministers in September–October 1945 and effectively ended co-operation. Truman and Churchill both regarded democracy as a matter of fundamental human rights rather than horse trading. In restating the fundamentals of US foreign policy in October 1945, Truman emphasised that 'all peoples . . . should be permitted to choose their own government'.[27] However, within the State Department a more flexible attitude was apparent as the professional diplomats wrestled with the reality of Soviet power. Bohlen revised his earlier opinion and suggested the recognition of 'legitimate Soviet security interests in Eastern Europe'[28] if this was the price of East–West co-operation. In December 1945 Secretary of State Byrnes met with Stalin in Moscow and 'sought not to challenge Soviet pre-eminence in Eastern Europe but to humanise it'.[29] Byrnes reached a compromise and left Moscow in a triumphant mood but his triumph was short-lived as Truman sharply rebuked him for accepting 'police states' in Eastern Europe.[30] Truman's commitment to democracy was absolute and he directed Byrnes to make no concessions without his direct authorisation, stating, 'unless Russia is faced with an iron fist and strong language another war is in the making', and concluding, 'I'm tired of babying the Soviets.'[31]

Truman was not just concerned about the future of Eastern Europe but was alarmed by Soviet claims to Iran and the Black Sea Straits which might have extended totalitarianism beyond Europe. He was uncertain of Soviet aims and suspected that expansion rather than security was Stalin's goal. After Stalin's speech of February 1946, which appeared to threaten future war, Truman sought the opinion of the American embassy in Moscow. Diplomat George Kennan's 'Long Telegram' of 22nd February 1946 put into words Truman's fears about the Soviet Union. Kennan bluntly condemned the Soviet Union as a highly insecure state, but it was his assessment that Russia was committed to 'constant pressure to extend the limits of Russian police power'[32] that galvanised the United States into confrontation and gave the Long Telegram its influential place in US foreign policy. This confirmed Truman's instinct that only stern resistance to the Soviet Union would prevent communist expansion. The withdrawal of the Soviet Union from Iran under direct US pressure in May 1946 seemed to prove the point.

A new 'get tough' policy was rapidly in evidence as the United States attached conditions to aid, ended reparations from Germany, refused to share nuclear technology and began to rebuild the German economy. In addition, a series of anti-Soviet press briefings began to alter press and public opinion that had given a hostile reception to Churchill's 'Iron Curtain' speech. In September 1946 *Newsweek* warned Americans, 'the Soviet Government has made up its mind that capitalism must be destroyed if communism is to live'.[33]

The battle lines were being drawn but not everyone in Truman's administration was convinced of the existence of a Soviet threat. Secretary for War Stimson had recommended sharing nuclear technology with the Soviet Union and Bohlen and Byrnes remained pragmatists. The main challenge, however, came from veteran Secretary of State for Commerce Henry Wallace who, from March to September 1946, directly questioned Truman's assumptions of Soviet expansionism. Wallace regarded Stalin's actions as defensive and stated 'that Russia wanted peace but was afraid of our intentions'.[34] Wallace expressed his opinions in public and in a direct criticism of Truman stated, 'the tougher we get, the tougher the Russians will get'.[35] Truman asked for his resignation on 20th September 1946 and confided in his diary, 'I do not understand a dreamer like that . . . the Reds, phonies and parlor pinks seem to be banded together and are becoming a national danger.'[36] This was indicative of Truman's absolute belief that Stalin was intent upon the expansion of communism, and four days after dismissing Wallace his opinions were reinforced by the Clifford Report, a 100,000-word analysis of all available intelligence data, which concluded that the Soviet Union was expansionist and targeting Turkey and Greece to gain access to the Mediterranean. In January 1947 Byrnes, aware that he did not enjoy Truman's full confidence, resigned and removed a moderate voice that spoke for co-operation and a 'two-world' system rather than confrontation.

The new secretary of state, George Marshall, was brisk and businesslike, anxious to settle the future of Germany and to address the restoration of European trade and employment. Kennan shared these aims as they seemed necessary in light of his analysis of the Soviet threat as one of propaganda aimed at promoting internal revolution in the poverty-stricken states of Europe rather than a direct military invasion. Marshall appointed Kennan to direct a new Policy Planning Unit but the question of financial assistance to Europe was dramatically overshadowed by events. In February 1947 Britain announced that financial aid to Greece and Turkey could no longer be maintained given the parlous state of the British economy. This immediately raised the spectre of communist expansion into the Mediterranean as highlighted in the Clifford Report and encouraged Congress to endorse substantial aid to Greece and Turkey after Truman raised the threat of totalitarianism.

The Truman Doctrine outlined on 12th March 1947 was a fault line in US policy that ended all prospects of co-operation and committed the United States to the world-wide confrontation of totalitarianism (which in essence meant communism). Truman's promise 'to support free peoples who are resisting attempted subjugation by armed minorities or outside pressure'[37] was global and universal, much to the dismay of Kennan and others who thought it would lead to 'everyone in the world coming to you with his palm out'.[38] Truman's policy was based on the false premise that the Soviet Union was actively supporting the Greek communists and by implication underwriting and directing communist movements world-wide. Yergin expressed the opinion that after the crisis in Greece, 'American leaders saw a Russian mastermind at work in every local crisis.'[39]

Marshall's concerns were more practical and on 15th April 1947 he met with Stalin to discuss the rebuilding of the German economy, but whereas Stalin counselled delay and patience Marshall expressed the concern that, 'the patient is sinking while the doctors deliberate'.[40] Marshall noted that Stalin doodled wolves' heads with a red pencil as he spoke, something Beaverbrook had also reported at Potsdam. If this indicated a sense of threat at the prospect of a restored Germany, Stalin never remarked on it.

The Moscow Conference of Foreign Ministers from March to April 1947 repeated the failure of the London Conference and after forty-three sterile sessions of talks both East and West contemplated the next step. The United States looked to the economic recovery of Europe, and in June 1947 the Marshall Plan offered financial assistance to the whole of Europe to answer Truman's concern that, 'totalitarian regimes are nurtured by misery and want'.[41] Marshall Aid was offered to the Soviet Union and Eastern Europe but it was linked to US trade, which Molotov rejected as a 'vicious American scheme for using dollars to buy its way'.[42]

All hope of future co-operation ended and Kennan, in an internal State Department strategy paper of July 1947, spoke of the need for 'firm but vigilant containment of Russian expansive tendencies' and coined the term 'containment' to describe the United States' policy towards the Soviet Union. Kennan was persuaded to publish the paper in the *Journal of Foreign Affairs*, under the none too deep anonymity of Mr 'X', and expounded a policy that sought to combat the Soviet Union through isolation.

There was as yet no US military commitment to Europe and if anything Truman was keen to encourage a third power, the 'United States of Europe', to stand between the Soviet Union and the United States. The proposal failed as France, with echoes of Soviet complaints, feared the revival of Germany, and Britain preferred to maintain close economic ties with the Commonwealth rather than Europe. All of this changed with the Czech Crisis of 1948 and the Berlin Crisis of 1948–49. The Czech Crisis evoked painful memories of Munich and appeasement ten years earlier. The lesson of Munich was not to appease dictators, and consequently Western Europe sought and obtained a US military commitment to Europe in NATO, formed in April 1949. This was a significant departure for US foreign policy and underlined the real fear of the 'red menace' that existed not just in the United States but in Western Europe. It was based on the simple premise that Stalin was planning the invasion of Western Europe. Truman, in his re-election campaign in November 1948, had extensively played the 'red card' and in his inaugural address of January 1949 he denounced communism as a false doctrine. The lifting of the Soviet blockade of Berlin in May 1949, due to the success of the Western airlift, confirmed to the West that Stalin only respected force. Germany was divided into two states: West Germany, founded in May 1949; and East Germany in October 1949. The division remained a potent symbol of Cold War confrontation until reunification in 1990.

By the end of 1949 containment appeared to be a successful policy as there had been no communist advances beyond Eastern Europe, but containment ended with the detonation of a Soviet nuclear bomb in July 1949 and the declaration of communism in China on 1st October 1949. The bomb removed the sense of security conferred by two oceans and made the United States feel vulnerable to attack – especially a surprise assault, a legacy of Pearl Harbor. Communism in

China had a long history as an independent movement but, 'Truman saw the Beijing regime for all practical purposes as an instrument of Moscow'.[43] There was a rush to defence and Kennan retired from office after disagreement with the more bellicose language of Truman's administration and the approval of an American H-bomb, which he believed was an unnecessary escalation of the arms race. Kennan was accused of displaying a 'Quaker' attitude and was replaced as director of the Policy Planning Unit by Paul Nitze.

Nitze was directed to review the threat posed by the Soviet Union against a background of increasing public fear of nuclear warfare and communist conspiracies. In January 1950 Senator Joseph McCarthy produced a list of 205 people he claimed were communist agents within the US Government seeking to undermine the security of the nation. McCarthy was eventually discredited but his charges electrified the nation and spawned a climate of intense war fever and extreme anti-communism to the extent that even the secretary-general of the United Nations was forced to declare that 'he was not and never had been a communist'.

Nitze's analysis of the Soviet threat, National Security Agency Paper NSC-68, was presented to Truman in April 1950, and it represented the abandonment of 'containment' in favour of outright military confrontation to counter a Soviet Union believed to be planning war, 'probably in the form of a surprise attack'.[44] The recommendation was for a tripling of the United States' defence budget with a major increase of the nuclear arsenal and a commitment to first use of the nuclear bomb to defend democracy. The financial implications led Truman immediately to shelve the report, but after the outbreak of war in Korea in June 1950 'American diplomacy, defence budgets and military reach exploded across the globe'.[45] The projected defence budget of 13.5 billion dollars in 1950 soared to 48.2 billion in 1951 and the result was world-wide military confrontation. General Douglas MacArthur, commander-in-chief of US forces in Korea, called for the use of the bomb and direct warfare against Communist China and publicly challenged Truman's more cautious prosecution of the war. Truman dismissed MacArthur, but out of 44,358 telegrams received by the White House, only 334 supported Truman, underlining the fear of communism in American society. MacArthur returned to New York to a ticker-tape reception and his speech to Congress in April 1951 left the United States in no doubt as to his assessment of the crisis: 'The communists in the Kremlin are engaged in a monstrous conspiracy to stamp out freedom all over the world.'[46]

It was in this climate and against a background of continuing war that the United States went to the polls in November 1952, and opted for security by electing General Eisenhower to the office of president. Eisenhower had made Korea a key election issue and to Truman's disgust he shared a platform with McCarthy and blamed communist successes upon 'Reds in Washington'.[47] One of Eisenhower's first acts was Executive Order 10450, an internal security programme against communist subversion that extended the confrontation of communism internally across every sphere of American life. Even the Pope declared 'that any Catholic who supported communism would be excommunicated'.[48]

The palpable fear of a communist threat to the world was also reflected in the media. *Life* magazine warned 'War can come and we will be ready',[49] and a collectable set of chewing-gum cards for children proclaimed: 'Fight the Red Menace.'[50] The conversion from co-operation to confrontation was total from the White House down to the child in the street. The United States was convinced that the Soviet Union intended to extend communism world-wide, by war if need be, and acted on that belief.

Overall, East–West co-operation was lost through Soviet intransigence but the communist world conspiracy that the United States confronted so vigorously was largely a chimera.

Questions

1. In what ways did Stalin's actions alienate the West?
2. How far did the Truman Doctrine make a prisoner of the foreign policy of the United States?

SOURCES

The following sources provide examples of the fears and confrontations that rapidly divided the superpowers.

1. MUTUAL SUSPICIONS AND OPPOSITION

Source A: Truman's 'iron fist'.

In December 1945 President Truman rebuked Secretary of State Byrnes for being too trusting of Stalin.

There isn't a doubt in my mind that Russia intends an invasion of Turkey and the seizure of the Black Sea Straits to the Mediterranean. Unless Russia is faced with an iron fist and strong language another war is in the making. Only one language do they understand – how many divisions have you? . . . I'm tired of babying the Soviets.

Source B: Stalin's Realpolitik.

In 1944 Milovan Djilas, a member of the Politburo of the Yugoslavian Communist Party, held talks with Stalin and recorded Stalin's attitude to occupied territories.

Stalin presented his views on the distinctive nature of the war that was being waged: This war is not as in the past; whoever occupies a territory also imposes on it his own social system. Everyone imposes his own system as far as his army has power to do so. It cannot be otherwise . . . Someone expressed doubt that the Germans would be able to recuperate within fifty years. But Stalin was of a different opinion. No, they will recover and very quickly. It is a highly developed industrial country with an extremely skilled and numerous working class and technical intelligentsia. Give them twelve to fifteen years and they'll be on their feet again . . . The war will soon be over. We shall recover in fifteen to twenty years, and then we'll have another go at it.

Source C: Truman Doctrine.

Truman's statement to Congress, 12th March 1947, concerning the communist threat to Greece and Turkey.

At the present moment in world history nearly every nation must choose between alternative ways of life. The choice is too often not a free one. One way of life is based upon the will of the majority and is distinguished by free institutions, guarantees of individual liberty, freedom of speech and religion and freedom from political oppression. The second way of life is based upon the will of the minority forcibly imposed upon the majority. It relies upon terror and oppression, a controlled press and radio, fixed elections and the suppression of personal freedoms. I believe it must be the policy of the United States to support free peoples who are resisting attempted subjugation by armed minorities or by outside pressures . . . The seeds of totalitarian regimes are nurtured by misery and want. They spread and grow in the evil soil of poverty and strife . . . The free peoples of the world look to us for support in maintaining their freedoms.

Source D: Cominform statement.

Malenkov, a member of the Soviet Politburo, condemned the Truman Doctrine at a meeting of the Cominform on 22nd September 1947.

The ruling clique of American imperialists ... has taken the path of outright expansion, of enslaving the weakened capitalist states of Europe and the colonial and independent countries. It has chosen the path of hatching new war plans against the Soviet Union and the new democracies ... The clearest and most specific expression of the policy ... is provided by the Truman–Marshall plans ... imitating the Hitlerites, the new aggressors are using blackmail and extortion.

Questions

1. What did Stalin mean by the phrase, 'the distinctive nature of the war that was being waged' (Source B)?
*2. How far do Sources B and D agree on the nature of the threat facing the Soviet Union?
3. How far is the sense of threat expressed in Sources A and C consistent?
4. How effective is the overall tone and language of the Truman Doctrine (Source C) in building a case for assistance to Greece and Turkey?
5. With reference to all four sources and to your own knowledge, comment on the similarities and differences between the nature of the threats perceived by Truman and Stalin.

Worked answer

*2. In Source B Stalin is speaking in 1944 at a time when the Second World War was in its closing stages, but despite the prospect of an Allied victory, Stalin is pessimistic about the future and states that once Germany has recovered from defeat, 'we'll have another go at it'. The threat perceived is very much of a hostile West and the renewal of war. He interprets the war not as a normal war, but as one between two opposing systems and consequently concludes that a future conflict is inevitable. This fear of a future war is also reflected in Source D when the Cominform statement accuses the West of 'hatching new war plans'. The language and tone of the statement, especially 'imperialists', 'outright expansion' and 'Hitlerites', also implies agreement on the ideological base of the conflict and very much reflects the concerns expressed by Stalin in Source B.

SOURCES

2. MUTUAL CONFRONTATION AND FEAR

Source E: Truman's response.

Truman's opinion of the Soviet blockade of Berlin, 1948.

The Berlin blockade was a move to test our capacity and will to resist. This action and the previous attempts to take over Greece and Turkey were part of a Russian plan to probe for soft spots in the Western Allies' positions all around their own perimeter.

Source F: Khrushchev's response.

Khrushchev's opinion of the Soviet blockade of Berlin, 1948.

At the very least adjustments to the [Potsdam] treaty were required as regarded the use of East German territory for access to West Berlin. Strictly for the sake of adhering to international law the West should have come to terms with us on this account. As it was, the West was putting its own very one-sided interpretation on the question of the GDR's right to control its borders. The problem had not been foreseen by the Potsdam agreement – an omission in the treaty which the West was turning to its own purposes.

Source G: Khrushchev on Korea.

In his memoirs Khrushchev recorded Stalin's limited support for the Korean War.

I remember Stalin had his doubts. He was worried that the Americans would jump in but we were inclined to think that if the war was fought swiftly – and Kim Il Sung was sure that it could be won swiftly – then intervention by the USA could be avoided . . . I must stress that the war wasn't Stalin's idea but Kim Il Sung's. Kim was the initiator. Stalin of course didn't try to dissuade him . . . Stalin called back all of our advisers who were with the North Korean divisions and regiments as well as all of the advisers who were serving as consultants and helping to build up the army. I asked Stalin about this, and he snapped back at me, 'It's too dangerous to keep our advisers there. They might be taken prisoner. We don't want there to be evidence for accusing us of taking part in this business. It's Kim Il Sung's affair.'

Source H: General MacArthur's resignation.

After his dismissal as commander-in-chief of US forces in Korea for insubordination MacArthur returned to a hero's welcome and justified his actions to Congress on 11th April 1951.

In the simplest terms what we are doing in Korea is this: we are trying to prevent a third world war . . . It is right for us to be in Korea. It was right last June. It is right today. I want to remind you why this is true. The communists in the Kremlin are engaged in a monstrous conspiracy to stamp out freedom all over the world. If they were to succeed the United States would be numbered among their principal victims. It must be clear to everyone that the United States cannot – and will not – sit idly by and await foreign conquest. The only question is: when is the best time to meet the threat and how? The best time to meet the threat is in the beginning. It is easier to put out a fire in the beginning when it is small than after it has become a roaring blaze.

Questions

1. What was the Western response to the Soviet blockade of Berlin?
2. In what ways do the views of Truman and Khrushchev in relation to the Berlin blockade differ (Sources E and F)?
3. How far does Source G convey a sense of doubt and uncertainty about the merits of Soviet involvement in the Korean War?
*4. To what extent is there agreement between Truman (Source E) and MacArthur (Source H) on the nature of the threat posed by the Soviet Union?
5. With reference to all of the sources and to your own knowledge, justify and explain the concerns of the United States.

Worked answer

*4. President Truman, in reacting to the Soviet blockade of Berlin (Source E), extends the Soviet threat beyond Berlin to any 'soft spot' on the Soviet perimeter in a clear implication that Berlin was not just an isolated threat but part of an overall Soviet strategy to advance communism world-wide. Truman's opening statement that the blockade was a test of 'our will to resist' demonstrates a determination to stand up to the Soviet Union and to combat the Soviet threat. General MacArthur takes a similar attitude to the war in Korea when he also looks beyond the immediate conflict and identifies a world-wide Soviet threat expressed as a 'monstrous conspiracy to stamp out freedom'. MacArthur is also determined to combat the Soviet threat and urges action with the words, 'cannot . . . sit idly by and await foreign conquest'. However, MacArthur's words identify a direct threat to the security of the United States whereas Truman refers to the Soviet threat as expansion around her own perimeter. Overall, both Truman and MacArthur share the same core ideas that the Soviet Union is expansionist and must be resisted, but they differ on the scale and nature of the threat.

3

PEACEFUL COEXISTENCE

BACKGROUND NARRATIVE

After the death of Stalin in March 1953 the Soviet Politburo avoided giving all power to a single individual and confirmed the collective leadership of Malenkov, Molotov, Beria, Bulganin and Khrushchev. A policy of destalinisation was introduced and in August 1953 Prime Minister Malenkov recommended a policy of 'peaceful coexistence' with the West. The new mood of openness and tolerance in Soviet society was reflected in the novel *Thaw*, published by Soviet writer Ilia Ehrenburg in 1954.

The leadership of the West also changed. Churchill was elected prime minister of Britain in 1951 and in a surprise reversal to his reputation as a Cold War warrior he pressed for a summit with the Soviet Union to end the Cold War.

However, in the United States the election of Eisenhower as president in November 1952 reflected a hardening of Cold War attitudes. The United States was traumatised by the Korean War, which ended in July 1953 with 32,629 Americans killed, 103,284 injured and the deaths of approximately 3 million Korean civilians. American anger was reflected in the policies of Secretary of State John Foster Dulles who recommended the 'rollback' of communism and 'massive retaliation' against the Soviet Union. The limitations of these policies were demonstrated by the lack of a US response to the Soviet suppression of protest in East Germany in 1953 and more significantly in Hungary in 1956. Eisenhower's Domino Theory, pronounced in 1954, and the Eisenhower Doctrine of 1957 extended US military alliances world-wide in an attempt firmly to contain communism.

The first summit since Potsdam in 1945 was held in Geneva in July 1955. In attendance were the leaders of the four Allied powers: Eisenhower, Eden, Faure and Malenkov. Churchill had retired in April 1955 before realising his last aim of a settlement with the Soviet Union. There was no agreement, but the friendly atmosphere was styled the 'Spirit of Geneva' and raised the possibility of future concord. In February 1956 Khrushchev dramatically extended destalinisation by condemning Stalin's rule in a closed meeting of the Communist Party, and in 1958 he emerged as the single leader of the Soviet Union.

The possibilities for peaceful coexistence were raised by the success of a second summit held at Camp David in September 1959. However, in May 1960, a Soviet walkout over the U2 spy plane incident ended the third summit in Paris and the hopes for peaceful coexistence. The Berlin Crisis of 1961 marked the return of the Cold War.

ANALYSIS (1): TO WHAT EXTENT DID PEACEFUL COEXISTENCE INTRODUCE A THAW IN THE COLD WAR?

The Soviet policy of peaceful coexistence was most associated with Khrushchev but it was the policy of the whole Soviet Politburo, and at its height in 1955–59 it precipitated a significant thaw in the Cold War. Khrushchev, in particular, travelled the world and gave communism a jovial, human face but peaceful coexistence was rejected by Mao Zedong, and to President Eisenhower it represented more words than deeds.

On 9th March 1953 Stalin was laid alongside Lenin in the Red Square Mausoleum. To guard against any future Stalins the Politburo endorsed a collective leadership that gave Malenkov control over the government and Khrushchev control over the Party. Within weeks a clear process of destalinisation was under way with the relaxation of Soviet rule in Eastern Europe and the Baltic States, release of private land to peasants and an amnesty for approximately 1 million prisoners. The arrest and execution of Beria, the feared head of the MVD, in June 1953 finally marked the end of Stalin's rule. However, there were limits to the new freedom, and in June 1953 a rising of East German workers in pursuit of free elections was ruthlessly suppressed.

After Stalin's funeral Malenkov launched a peace initiative, stating, 'we stand as we have always stood for the peaceful coexistence of the two systems'.[1] This represented a denial of the Marxist theory of inevitable conflict with capitalism and provoked controversy within the Politburo and criticism from Mao Zedong.

The first signs of a thaw were the end of the Korean War in July 1953, the settlement of border disputes with Turkey and Iran and the recognition of Israel. Malenkov also offered an olive branch to the United States with the words, 'there is no dispute or outstanding issue which cannot be settled peacefully'.[2]

To the surprise of many, it was Churchill who gave the most enthusiastic response to peaceful coexistence and he appealed for an East–West summit to end the Cold War. Churchill met with Eisenhower on 1st December 1953 in Bermuda to discuss relations with the Soviet Union, but to his dismay Eisenhower ruled out a summit and described the new Soviet Union as nothing but a tart, 'despite bath, perfume or lace it was still the same old girl'.[3]

The United States was preoccupied with the fear of communist expansion as Communist China threatened the Chinese Nationalist-held islands of Quemoy and Matsu and supported Ho Chi Minh's communist movement in French Indochina. Instead of peaceful coexistence Eisenhower feared the relentless advance of communism through Asia. This was dramatically expressed in the Domino Theory of April 1954: 'you have a row of dominoes set up and you knock over the first one . . . '[4] To counter the advance of communism, Secretary of State John Foster Dulles proposed a policy of 'massive atomic and thermonuclear retaliation',[5] but the successful test of the first Soviet H-bomb in August 1953, a peace settlement in Indochina in July 1954 and Churchill's continued insistence that 'jaw jaw is better than war war'[6] encouraged Eisenhower to explore peaceful coexistence.

Eisenhower had spoken of the need for Soviet deeds not words and in April 1955 the Soviet Union proposed a formal peace treaty with Austria. This was successful and led to full independence for Austria on 15th May 1955. In a further success for peaceful co-existence Khrushchev and Bulganin visited Yugoslavia in May 1955, and despite a very cold reception endorsed Tito's leadership and ended years of hostility.

Consequently, by spring 1955 peaceful coexistence had significantly reduced East–West tension and the Soviet Union proposed a summit. The Geneva Summit of June 1955 was the first meeting of Allied leaders since Potsdam but it arrived too late for Churchill, who had retired through ill health in April 1955. The Soviet delegation was led by Prime Minister Bulganin, who had replaced Malenkov in February 1955, but as Anthony Eden recorded, 'the authority of Khrushchev could always be felt'.[7] The key issue for the Soviet Union and the ultimate test of peaceful coexistence was the future of Germany. Marshall Aid had revitalised West Berlin into an island of capitalism in the middle of East Germany and West Germany had been rearmed and admitted to NATO in May 1955. The West refused Soviet requests for the recognition of East Germany and rejected proposals for a unified but disarmed Germany. Khrushchev blamed Dulles for the lack of progress and complained, 'that vicious cur Dulles was always prowling around Eisenhower, snapping at him if he got out of line'.[8] However, the 'Spirit of Geneva' in terms of friendly exchanges held out the prospect of future agreement. Eisenhower's contribution to peaceful coexistence was to propose an 'Open Skies' treaty allowing the aerial inspection of each other's territory, but the United States had most to gain and Khrushchev dismissed it as 'nothing more than a bold espionage plot'.[9] In secret, Eisenhower had already authorised U2 missions over the Soviet Union. According to Eden, the success of Geneva was the relaxation of tension and the realisation 'that no country attending wanted war'.[10]

The Soviet newspaper *Izvestia* reported, 'A new era in international relations has begun'[11] and this appeared to be confirmed by open exchanges and visits between American and Soviet scientists, the return of the seaport Porkkala to Finland, the reduction of the Red Army by 600,000 troops and the Soviet recognition of West Germany. However, the most significant break with the past came with Khrushchev's speech to a closed session of the Twentieth Congress of the Communist Party on 25th February 1956. Khrushchev shocked the delegates with an open denunciation of Stalin. This was a new, confident Soviet Union, casting off Stalinism, celebrating record harvests and economic growth and reaching out to the world with popular visits by Khrushchev and Bulganin in the spring of 1956 to Burma, India, Afghanistan and Britain. In Bombay Khrushchev gave considerable hope for the future by stating, 'the socialists and the capitalists have to live side by side on one planet'.[12] In London there were regular overflights of the new Soviet passenger jet the TU-104 in a triumphant display of Soviet technology only a year after Khrushchev had expressed his embarrassment at travelling to the Geneva Summit in a twin-engine Ilyushin. Khrushchev was convinced that communism would prove attractive to the Third World and would in the long term overtake capitalism.

However, Soviet confidence was shattered in October 1956 by widespread protests in Poland and Hungary for greater political freedom. Events in Poland were settled peaceably with the replacement of the Soviet leadership with popular Polish communist leaders but in Hungary protest turned to open revolt. The Red Army crushed the revolt with the deaths of some 30,000 protesters and the Hungarian prime minister, Imre Nagy, was imprisoned and executed in a harsh display of the limits of Soviet tolerance. The reaction of the West was muted by the Suez Crisis when Britain and France also resorted to military force and invaded Egypt on 29th October 1956 to defend their national interests.

The Hungarian Rising and the controversy surrounding Khrushchev's condemnation of Stalin produced an anti-Khrushchev coalition in the Politburo and in June 1957 the Politburo voted 7 to 4 to dismiss him as party leader. However, in a bold appeal to the wider party Khrushchev survived the challenge to his leadership and Malenkov, his chief opponent, was banished to Mongolia as the director of a power plant. Prime Minister Bulganin was also forced to resign and Khrushchev assumed total authority over the Party and government.

However, the criticisms of Khrushchev also exposed the limited success of peaceful coexistence in moderating US hostility. The Eisenhower Doctrine of March 1957 echoed the Truman Doctrine and guaranteed assistance 'against armed aggression from any country controlled by international communism'.[13] The successful launch of Sputnik in October 1957 was a triumph for Soviet technology but it also intimidated the United States and provoked a hostile response. George Kennan, when delivering the Reith Lectures in Oxford in November 1957, stated, 'the Russia of Khrushchev was not the Russia of Stalin'[14] but Eisenhower remained very sceptical of peaceful coexistence.

The deteriorating situation in East Germany preoccupied Khrushchev as an estimated 2.2 million skilled workers had fled to the more prosperous West Germany via the open border in Berlin. In November 1958 he expressed the concern that 'Berlin is a smouldering fuse that has been connected to a powder keg'[15] and demanded an immediate Western withdrawal from Berlin.

The opportunity for a breakthrough arose in September 1959 when Khrushchev accepted an invitation to Camp David. Secretary of State Dulles, whom Khrushchev believed 'lived and breathed hatred of communism'[16] had died from abdominal cancer in May 1959, and his absence raised the possibility of agreement. Khrushchev's visit was a significant success and the American public warmed to the communist leader who wanted to visit Disney World. The press spoke of the 'Spirit of Camp David' and a formal summit meeting was agreed for Paris in May 1960. However, Khrushchev blundered at a press conference when he boasted, 'We will bury you.' He was speaking in the context of economic competition but his words rekindled the US sense of threat.

By 1960 Khrushchev was under significant pressure for a diplomatic success as the Politburo was increasingly critical of his domestic policies. The ploughing of virgin lands had created an ecological disaster, the targets of the sixth Five Year Plan were abandoned as unrealistic and the reforms of the party administration and education were spectacular failures. In addition Mao Zedong was increasingly critical of peaceful coexistence, with regular articles in the Chinese *Red Flag* magazine praising the works of Lenin in veiled attacks against Soviet revisionism.

On 1st May 1960 the Soviet Air Force successfully shot down one of the regular American U2 spy planes over the Soviet Union and granted Khrushchev a propaganda triumph he could not ignore. The Paris Summit ended with a Soviet walkout in protest at Eisenhower's refusal to apologise or to ban future U2 flights. It was a much needed boost to Khrushchev's prestige and with a new president of the United States on the horizon there was an assumption that negotiations could wait.

In July 1960 the dispute with China burst into the open as Khrushchev condemned Chinese communism following Mao Zedong's complaint that 'peaceful coexistence was a bourgeois pacifist concept'.[17] Khrushchev never trusted China, and in a bizarre adoption of US rhetoric accused the Chinese of a 'desire to rule the world'.[18]

Khrushchev's negotiations with the United States were resumed in June 1961 at a summit with President Kennedy in Vienna. The exodus of East German workers through the 'escape hatch' of West Berlin had reached a crisis point of 4000 people per day and Khrushchev threatened military action to force an immediate Western withdrawal from Berlin. Kennedy refused to be intimidated. In frustration Khrushchev resorted to unilateral action and on the night of 13th August 1961 Soviet workers began the construction of the Berlin Wall to close the thirty-mile gap in the Iron Curtain. Peaceful coexistence evaporated as Soviet and US tanks faced each other in central Berlin. Eleven weeks later, on 31st October 1961, the body of Stalin was removed from the Red Square Mausoleum and buried alongside the Kremlin Wall under several tons of concrete in a final break with the past.

Overall, peaceful coexistence produced a significant thaw in the Cold War and its failure to produce a lasting political settlement represented a lost opportunity for the West.

Questions

1. How successful was Khrushchev in transforming the image of the Soviet Union?

2. What held the West back from fully embracing peaceful coexistence? What was needed to produce a breakthrough?

ANALYSIS (2): WHY DID PEACEFUL COEXISTENCE NOT SUCCEED IN ENDING THE COLD WAR?

After 1950, the rise of Red China turned the Cold War into a triangular conflict and China increasingly pursued an independent policy at odds with peaceful coexistence. In addition, the United States was highly concerned that the Soviet Union would take advantage of the political vacuum in the Third World to promote and expand communism as Britain and France retreated from empire.

On 4th November 1952 the newly elected President Eisenhower fulfilled his campaign pledge 'to go to Korea' in a symbolic gesture of his determination to end the Korean War. The intervention of Communist Chinese troops had produced a stalemate and many Americans favoured all-out war against Communist China, including the use of nuclear weapons if necessary to achieve victory. The mood in the United States was belligerent, with a belief that the free world was engaged in a struggle for survival. Secretary of State John Foster Dulles appeared on television in January 1953 and promised 'all those suffering under communist slavery . . . you can count on us'.[19] The overt deployment of nuclear weapons on Okinawa in May 1953, in striking range of Communist China, raised a general fear of nuclear war.

In July 1953 the new Soviet leadership of Malenkov and Khrushchev brokered a peace settlement and ended the Korean War in the first act of peaceful coexistence. However, a significant dispute remained as the United States refused to recognise the government of Mao Zedong and blocked the admission of Communist China to the United Nations while continuing to recognise Jiang Jieshi and his Nationalist army as the legitimate government of China. Jiang Jieshi had been defeated in the Chinese Civil War of 1946–49 and occupied the offshore islands of Formosa, Quemoy and Matsu under the protection of the US Pacific Fleet. This simmering dispute between Communist China and the United States mitigated against Chinese acceptance of peaceful co-existence as China expected robust Soviet diplomatic and military support to force a change in US policy.

The United States identified a seamless communist world that stretched in an arc from Berlin to Saigon with the threat of unlimited communist expansion. Dulles was sceptical of peaceful coexistence and expressed the view that Lenin and Stalin might be dead, 'but their doctrine is not dead',[20] and he was determined not only to prevent further communist expansion but to 'roll back' communism wherever possible. Consequently, as the Soviet Union was promoting peaceful coexistence, the United States was placing its faith in the nuclear deterrent to force concessions or even victory in the Cold War.

Nuclear deterrence formed the basis of Eisenhower's 'New Look' defence policy of 1953. Eisenhower described the bomb as a weapon that should be 'used just exactly as we use a bullet or anything else'.[21] Secretary of Defense Wilson summarised the approach as 'more bang for the buck', meaning a reduction in costs and American casualties by deploying the bomb rather than GIs in future conflicts. In January 1954 Dulles confirmed 'massive retaliation' as the US defence strategy to deter 'the mighty land power of the communist world'.[22] The United States was mesmerised by the size of the Chinese and Soviet armies and believed that only the threat of the nuclear bomb would prevent communism sweeping through Asia and Europe. The focus of attention was Indochina and in April 1954 Eisenhower's Domino Theory predicted the 'fall of all Southeast Asia to communists'[23] in an alarmist image of unstoppable communist expansion.

To some extent, Eisenhower was a prisoner of American public opinion as Senator McCarthy was at the height of his influence in 1953–54 and any toleration of communism would have been political suicide. McCarthy initiated investigations into every area of American life to uncover communist conspirators. Some 10 million Americans were investigated for communist sympathies, the US Communist Party was banned, a government loyalty oath was instituted and books by communist authors were removed from library shelves (as was a book about Robin Hood, which the Indiana State Library Board cited as likely to encourage communism).

In June 1953 the limitations of US power and Dulles's policy of 'roll back' were exposed when the Soviet Union crushed the workers' rising in East Germany. The absence of any intervention by the West was a tacit recognition of the Soviet Bloc. This inaction was repeated in 1956 when the Soviet Union also crushed the Hungarian Rising. Likewise, the Soviet Union took no action when the United States sponsored and supported coups against the left-leaning governments of Iran in 1953 and Guatemala in 1954.

However, the major test of US policy arose over Indochina when the communist Vietminh successfully besieged a French garrison at Dien Bien Phu in May 1954. The French requested US military assistance and Nathan Twining, the US Airforce chief of staff, advised, 'three small A-bombs placed properly . . . would have taught those Chinese a good lesson'.[24] Eisenhower resisted the call to 'massive retaliation', conscious of the existence of the Soviet H-Bomb and France was subsequently defeated.

The victory for the Vietminh sustained military force, and consequently Mao Zedong criticised peaceful coexistence and dismissed the US nuclear threat as a 'paper tiger'. Mao requested Soviet nuclear weapons but Khrushchev distrusted China and was 'firmly opposed to granting such weapons to the less restrained Chairman Mao'.[25]

At the Geneva Peace Conference of July 1954 Indochina was divided into Vietnam, Laos and Cambodia. Vietnam was divided at the 17th Parallel between the communist North and the democratic South in an interim arrangement pending elections. However, when opinion polls showed that the Vietminh would win 80 per cent of the vote, the leader of South Vietnam, Ngo Dinh Diem, cancelled the elections with US support. The defence of democracy in Asia meant that the United States supported the corrupt dictatorships of Diem in Vietnam, Rhee in South Korea and Jiang Jieshi in Formosa. The irony was not lost on the Soviet Union, given the United States' repeated demands for elections in Eastern Europe.

The end of the war in Indochina in 1954 and the 'Spirit of Geneva' of 1955 boosted the prospects for peaceful coexistence but as the military threats faded the new battleground became military and economic aid to the Third World. Khrushchev stated, 'there can be no such thing as ideological peaceful coexistence'[26] and he embarked on a series of successful overseas visits to promote communism. He believed that people in the Third World would choose communism after decades of colonial and capitalist exploitation and that 'progress is on our side and victory will inevitably be ours'.[27] The Soviet challenge came at a vulnerable time for the West. France and Britain were withdrawing from empire in Africa, the Middle East and Asia, and the United States feared a political vacuum open to Soviet blandishments and communist expansion. Soviet propaganda in the Third World was assisted by the Suez Crisis of 1956 and after 1955 by Martin Luther King's campaign for equal rights for Black people in the American South. The United States' commitment to human rights seemed hollow when Black Americans were denied the right to vote, hundreds of paratroopers were needed in 1957 to allow Black children to enter Little Rock High School in Arkansas, and in 1958 a nine-year-old Black boy received a fourteen-year prison sentence for kissing a seven-year-old white girl in North Carolina.

To counter the advance of Soviet diplomacy, the United States attempted to dominate each region and deny communism opportunities for expansion. In the wake of the Indochina War Asia was secured against communism by the formation of the South East Asia Treaty Organisation (SEATO) in September 1954. The Organisation of American States (OAS), formed in 1948, protected South America against communist penetration, and after 1949 the North Atlantic Treaty Organisation (NATO) policed Europe.

The weak spot was the Middle East following the end of British and French colonial rule, and as the Middle East supplied 89 per cent of Western oil, it became the focus of US attention. In May 1953 Dulles attempted to interest Egypt's President Nasser in an alliance, but Nasser regarded Israel and Britain as the enemy, and with regard to the Soviet Union stated, 'we've never had any trouble with them . . . but the British have been here for 70 years'.[28] Nasser was determined to champion the Arab cause against Israel and when arms from the West were denied he took advantage of the Cold War rivalry and obtained arms from Czechoslovakia in September 1955. After the debacle of Suez in 1956 Western influence was sharply reduced and Eisenhower announced the Eisenhower Doctrine in January 1957 to combat Soviet involvement in the region. Congress was hostile to Eisenhower's request for an immediate assistance of 200 million dollars as there was no evidence of a communist threat to the Middle East. In response to persistent questioning from Senator Fulbright, Eisenhower and Dulles were forced to admit, 'the communist threat was difficult to define or substantiate'.[29] Eisenhower eventually conceded that the aim was to erect a large 'keep out' notice to the Soviet Union to prevent intended future expansion. The Central Treaty Organisation (CENTO) Pact of 1958 served this purpose by linking the key Middle Eastern states into a defence alliance and, much to Soviet disquiet, completed the world-wide encirclement of the Soviet Union.

On 4th October 1957 the United States was stunned by the successful launch of Sputnik. To the Soviet Union, it was a triumph of Soviet technology and a possible lever to encourage concessions from the United States. However, in the United States it raised the fear of a nuclear-missile strike and resulted in a rush to build nuclear-bomb shelters. Dr Edward Teller, the father of the United States H-bomb told television audiences, 'America has lost a battle more important and greater than Pearl Harbor.'[30] Peaceful coexistence was irreparably damaged and the immediate results were the formation of NASA in 1958 and the extension of the Cold War into space. However, Eisenhower, to his credit, resisted the demands for a massive increase in defence spending and questioned the extent of the 'missile gap'.

In 1958 in a further rebuff to peaceful coexistence Communist China started shelling the Nationalist-held islands of Quemoy and Matsu in pursuit of an overall victory against Jiang Jieshi's nationalists. A similar attack in March 1955 was ended when the United States threatened to use nuclear weapons to defend the Nationalist island bases in a successful application of the doctrine of 'massive retaliation'. Eisenhower renewed full US support to Jiang Jieshi, whereas the Soviet Union angered Communist China by refusing the protection of its nuclear umbrella. Consequently, Communist China was forced to abandon plans for invasion in favour of intermittent shelling, and began its own nuclear-weapons research programme. The breach with the Soviet Union deepened as Khrushchev engaged in a friendly summit with Eisenhower at Camp David in 1959, an accord that Mao Zedong condemned as an endorsement of capitalism.

The U2 spy plane incident in 1960 extinguished the 'Spirit of Camp David' and on 17th January 1961 Eisenhower gave his farewell address to the nation as John F. Kennedy became president of the United States. Eisenhower's words demonstrated that peaceful coexistence had made little impact on US perceptions of the Soviet Union: 'we face a hostile ideology, global in scope ... ruthless in purpose and insidious in method'.[31]

In August 1961 the Soviet Union was humbled as the Berlin Wall was constructed to save East Germany from ignominious economic collapse. Peaceful coexistence had failed to attract Western concessions, particularly a settlement of divided Germany and as the wall rose peaceful coexistence collapsed.

Ultimately, peaceful coexistence failed against Communist China's commitment to military force and the United States' conviction of a Soviet threat in Asia, the Third World and space.

Questions

1. In what ways did peaceful coexistence alter the nature of the Soviet challenge to the West?
2. How significant was the rise of Communist China to the rejection of peaceful coexistence?

SOURCES

1. PEACEFUL COEXISTENCE

Source A: Prime Minister Eden at Geneva.

In his memoirs Eden recorded his impression of the summit talks with President Eisenhower, Prime Minister Faure and Soviet Party Secretary Khrushchev, July 1955.

Every country present learnt that no country attending wanted war and each understood why. The Russians realised, as we did, that this situation had been created by the deterrent power of thermo-nuclear weapons. Accordingly, they were determined to keep a free hand to develop these weapons as far and as fast as their country's very considerable resources would take them . . . The communist powers would continue to prosecute their purpose by every means. To do this they would work in areas, and by methods, including the use of conventional weapons, which they believed would not entail retaliation by nuclear weapons.

Source B: Khrushchev at Geneva.

In his memoirs Khrushchev recorded his impressions of the Western powers.

We returned to Moscow from Geneva knowing we hadn't achieved any concrete results. But we were encouraged, realising now that our enemies probably feared us as much as we feared them. They rattled their sabers and tried to pressure us into agreements which were more profitable for them because they were frightened of us . . . They realised that they would have to build their relations with us on new assumptions and new expectations if they really wanted peace. The Geneva meeting was an important breakthrough for us on the diplomatic front. We had established ourselves as able to hold our own in the international arena.

Source C: massive retaliation.

The US Secretary of State John Foster Dulles announced the strategy of massive retaliation on 12th January 1954.

The Soviet communists are planning for what they call 'an entire historical era' and we should do the same. They seek, through many types of maneuvers, gradually to divide and weaken the free nations by overextending them in efforts, which, as Lenin put it, are 'beyond their strength, so that they come to practical bankruptcy.'... Local defense will always be important. But there is no local defense which will alone contain the mighty land power of the communist world. Local defenses must be reinforced by the further deterrent of massive retaliatory power.

Source D: Khrushchev and peaceful coexistence.

In his memoirs Khrushchev defined the concept of peaceful coexistence.

There is a battle going on in the world to decide who will prevail over whom: will the working class prevail or the bourgeoisie ... We Communists, we Marxist–Leninists, believe that progress is on our side and victory will inevitably be ours. Yet the capitalists won't give an inch and still swear to fight to the bitter end. Therefore how can we talk of peaceful coexistence with capitalist ideology? Peaceful coexistence between different systems of government is possible but peaceful coexistence among different ideologies is not ... I have always said there can be no such thing as ideological peaceful coexistence.

Source E: Chinese dissent.

Khrushchev recorded in his memoirs the disputes with the Chinese leadership over peaceful coexistence.

Mao Tse-tung also declared that peaceful coexistence was a bourgeois pacifist notion. Since then China has recklessly slandered the Communist Party of the Soviet Union for its policy of peaceful coexistence ... There is, however, one thing I know for sure about Mao. He's a nationalist and at least when I knew him he was bursting with an impatient desire to rule the world. His plan was to rule China, then Asia, then what?

Source F: Communist Control.

The United States Communist Control Act, 24th August 1954, banned the US Communist Party.

The Congress hereby finds and declares that the Communist Party of the United States, although purportedly a political party, is in fact an instrumentality of a conspiracy to overthrow the Government of the United States. It constitutes an authoritarian dictatorship within a republic, demanding for itself the rights and privileges accorded to political parties, but denying all others the liberties guaranteed by the Constitution ... the policies and programs of the Communist Party are secretly prescribed for it by the foreign leaders of the world communism movement ... Holding that doctrine, its role as an agency of a hostile foreign power renders its existence a clear present and continuing danger to the security of the United States.

Questions

1. In the context of Source D what is meant by the phrase, 'progress is on our side'?
2. What evidence is there in Sources A and C to show that Eden and Dulles shared a belief in the importance of nuclear weapons?
3. How far are Eden's fears of a new communist challenge confirmed by Khrushchev in Source B?
4. How far apart are China and the Soviet Union in their attitudes to relations with the West as indicated by Sources D and E?
*5. What underlying fears unite the views expressed in Sources A, C and F?
6. Considering all of the above sources and your own know-ledge, explain how peaceful coexistence altered the nature of the Soviet challenge and the responses of Communist China and the United States?

Worked answer

*5. The consistent underlying fear expressed in Sources A, C and F is of an expansionist, hostile Soviet Union that is seeking to undermine the free world to achieve a goal of world communism. Eden in Source A is concerned about the prospect of communist infiltration and small-scale conventional wars that individually would not warrant a nuclear response but collectively would represent a significant expansion of communism. This fear is reflected in his statement that the Soviet Union was determined 'to prosecute their purpose by every means' and the implication is for constant vigilance.

This fear is supported by Dulles in Source C, where his words, 'through many types of maneuvers' echoes Eden's words and his belief that communism will be advanced step by step, 'to divide and weaken the free nations'. There is no doubt that he fears constant Soviet pressure on small nations to advance communism with the overall Soviet goal an 'entire historical era', or world communism. It is this underlying fear that prompts Dulles to confront the Soviet Union with the nuclear deterrent and the threat of 'massive retaliatory power'.

Source F refers to the internal threat of a communist 'conspiracy to overthrow the Government of the United States' and this fear of infiltration reflects the concerns expressed by Eden and Dulles of communism expanding in unconventional ways. The American Communists are believed to be directed 'by the foreign leaders of the world communist movement' and this confirms the underlying fear of a world-wide communist threat.

Overall, there is a strong measure of agreement between Sources A, C and F on the nature and tactics of world communism and a fear that without the nuclear deterrent and vigorous opposition communism will succeed in spreading world-wide.

SOURCES

2. THE U2 INCIDENT

Source G: Soviet protest.

The Soviet Union issued a note of protest on 10th May 1960, after the interception of a USAF U2 flight over the Soviet Union.

On May 1 of this year at 5 hours 36 minutes, Moscow time, a military aircraft violated the boundary of the Union of Soviet Socialist Republics . . . it was shot down by Soviet rocket troops in the area of Sverdlovsk . . . a new announcement was made by the US State Department on May 7 which contained the forced admission that the aircraft was sent into the Soviet Union for military reconnaissance purposes and, by that very fact, it was admitted that the flight was pursuing aggressive purposes.

Source H: Eisenhower's defence.

President Eisenhower defended U2 flights over the Soviet Union on 25th May 1960.

Aerial photography has been one of the many methods we have used to keep ourselves and the free world abreast of major Soviet military developments . . . The plain truth is this: when a nation needs intelligence activity, there is no time when vigilance can be relaxed. Incidentally, from Pearl Harbor we learned that even negotiation itself can be used to conceal preparations for a surprise attack . . . Here in our country anyone can buy maps and aerial photographs showing our cities, our dams, our plants, our highways – indeed our whole industrial and economic complex. We know that Soviet attachés regularly collect this information. Last fall Chairman Khrushchev's train passed no more than a few hundred feet from an operational ICBM in plain view from his window . . . This is as it should be. We are proud of our freedom.

Questions

1. How does the tone and language of Source G indicate a propaganda victory for the Soviet Union?
*2. In what ways does President Eisenhower (Source H) justify the U2 flights?
3. Considering both Sources G and H and your wider knowledge of the Cold War, why did the U2 incident mark a return to confrontation?

Worked answer

*2. President Eisenhower's statement is largely defensive in tone but he nevertheless sets out a number of clear justifications for the U2 flights. First, he expresses the need to 'keep . . . abreast of major Soviet military developments' which, by implication, are a threat to the 'free world' and must be kept under constant surveillance. Second, he raises the fear of another Pearl Harbor and emphasises his determination to ensure that the United States never again suffers a surprise attack. Third, Eisenhower cites the openness of American society, where 'anyone can buy maps' and by implication criticises the more secretive and closed Soviet Union, where military activities are concealed. By stating that 'Soviet attachés regularly collect this information', he is indicating that the U2 flights merely make things even in the intelligence war. Consequently, Eisenhower's overall justification of the U2 flights is as a defensive measure to ensure the safety of the United States.

4

THE MISSILE RACE

BACKGROUND NARRATIVE

On 4th October 1957 the Soviet Union successfully launched Sputnik, the world's first artificial satellite, into Earth orbit and sparked a missile race with the United States.

Sputnik crossed the United States four times and raised the possibility of an intercontinental ballistic missile (ICBM) strike against American cities. The United States was isolated from the Soviet Union by two oceans and protected by a superior navy and air force, but there was no defence against an attack from space.

The launch of Sputnik 2, on 3rd November 1957, confirmed the Soviet lead in missile technology and also, much to the criticism of animal welfare groups, carried the first dog into space: a husky called Laika. The CIA Gaither Report of 7th November 1957 warned President Eisenhower of an impending 'missile gap' and the need for the United States to take decisive action to counter the Soviet threat.

The confidence of the United States was further shaken on 7th December 1957 when, in a televised launch, a Vanguard rocket exploded on takeoff at Cape Canaveral in an embarrassing failure dubbed 'Phutnik' by the *Daily Mirror*.

On 1st February 1958 the United States successfully launched Explorer 1 into space but the Soviet Union kept up its technological challenge with Sputnik 3 in May 1958, the first rocket to the moon in 1959 and the first man into space, Yuri Gagarin, in April 1961.

However, in a less dramatic but highly significant development, the United States test fired the world's first submarine-launched ballistic missile (SLBM), the Polaris A1, in July 1960 from the nuclear-powered submarine *George Washington*. This development completed the nuclear triad of bombers, missiles and submarines as the principal delivery systems of nuclear weapons.

The ability of both superpowers to sustain and launch nuclear strikes ended the doctrine of 'massive retaliation' in recognition that a future war would mean mutually assured destruction (MAD).

On 14th October 1962 the missile race dominated world headlines when U2 reconnaissance photographs of Cuba revealed the construction of missile sites. The Soviet Union was attempting to gain an advantage in the nuclear-missile race but to the United States it was tantamount to war and the resulting crisis took the world to the brink of nuclear war.

ANALYSIS (1): WHY AND TO WHAT ADVANTAGE DID THE SOVIET UNION INITIATE THE MISSILE RACE?

The Soviet Union was intimidated by the United States' post-war nuclear monopoly and sought at least parity, if not a military and diplomatic advantage by directly targeting the United States with nuclear missiles. The related conquest of space, symbolised by Sputnik in 1957 and Yuri Gagarin in 1961, was also a triumph for Soviet technology, but the Soviet advantage was soon eclipsed by the superior resources of the United States.

The missile race was an extension of the race to develop nuclear weapons. At Potsdam, July 1945, President Truman ambiguously referred to the development of a new weapon of 'special destructive force' in a move calculated to neutralise the Soviet military advantage in Europe. Stalin interpreted the lack of full Allied disclosure of nuclear technology as a threat to the security of the Soviet Union and immediately directed the Soviet physicist Igor Kurchatov to 'provide us with the atomic bomb in the shortest possible time'.[1]

Stalin had directed few resources into nuclear research during the war years, given the high costs and energy requirements of researching nuclear fission, and consigned the Soviet rocket specialist Sergei Korolev to the Gulag for neglecting aircraft design. Both mistakes were corrected, and under the direction of Beria and the MVD nuclear weapons and missile research were accorded the highest priority.

The race for nuclear parity had begun but it was a race many American scientists wanted to avoid in favour of international controls over nuclear research. Samuel Allison, who counted down the Operation Trinity test explosion of the world's first nuclear bomb in July 1945, warned that in the absence of international co-operation the physicists would abandon nuclear research and 'devote themselves to studying the colors of butterfly wings'.[2] The Baruch Plan of June 1946 attempted to vest control over nuclear weapons in the United Nations but a Pandora's box had been opened and Stalin was fearful that the United States, with tried and tested technology, could resume nuclear-weapon production at will.

General Groves, who had directed the Manhattan Project in 1942–45, assured Congress that it would take the Soviet Union fifteen to twenty years to develop the nuclear bomb. To guarantee nuclear supremacy, all nuclear secrets were classified as top secret in the McMahon Act of August 1946.

In July 1949 the Soviet Union ended the United States' nuclear monopoly with the detonation of the first Soviet bomb, aided in part by Klaus Fuchs, a scientist in the Manhattan Project who passed nuclear secrets to the Soviet Union. The United States was unnerved by the Soviet success, the unmasking of a nuclear spy ring and the Soviet challenge in Berlin in 1948–49, which increased fears of Soviet expansionism. After the additional shock of the establishment of Communist China in October 1949, President Truman overruled misgivings on the National Security Council in January 1950 and authorised a full programme of hydrogen-bomb research. The outbreak of the Korean War in April 1950 accelerated the research in a race for the ultimate deterrent. The H-bomb utilised the science of nuclear fusion which, ounce for ounce, promised an explosive yield three times as great as nuclear fission. On 1st November 1952 the United States detonated its first experimental H-bomb but the advantage was short-lived as the Soviet H-bomb followed on 12th August 1953.

H-bomb technology was finally perfected by 1st March 1954, when the United States tested an operational-sized bomb in the Bikini Atoll in the South Pacific with an explosive yield equivalent to 15 million tons of TNT (compared to an equivalent of 20,000 tons for the bomb that devastated Hiroshima).

Pandora's box was empty. By 1955 the superpowers were balanced in nuclear-bomb technology but not in delivery systems. The United States could strike the Soviet Union from military bases in Britain, Greece, Turkey, Italy, Germany and Japan but the Soviet Union had no similar capability. In addition the United States had invested heavily in jet-aircraft development and in 1955 deployed the B52 Stratofortress: the first bomber with intercontinental range. The Soviet

Union copied the design with the TU20 Bear in 1956, but was unable to match Strategic Air Command (SAC), the principal nuclear strike arm of the United States, which maintained B52 bombers on twenty-four-hour alert.

The US threat of 'massive retaliation' was taken very seriously by Khrushchev and he looked to missiles for a counter-force: 'only by building up a nuclear missile force could we keep the enemy from unleashing war against us'.[3] Khrushchev also expected to gain a position of strength to pursue concessions from the West over the future of Berlin and Germany and to demonstrate Soviet power to the uncommitted nations of the Third World.

The Soviet lead in missile development reflected a long history of space research, with Russian scientist Konstantin Tsiolkovsky predicting rocket technology and the conquest of space as early as 1903. The Soviet Union conducted rocket tests during the 1930s but it was Nazi Germany, with the exigencies of war, that produced the scientific breakthrough and the successful development of V1 and V2 rockets. After the Second World War both superpowers put captured Nazi rocket scientists to work and developed medium-range, surface-to-surface missiles based on the V2 design. The United States deployed 'Thor' in Britain and 'Jupiter' in Italy and Turkey, whereas the Soviet Union deployed the less imaginatively named SS1, 2, 3, 4 and 5 along their Western border.

An early warning of the Soviet focus on missile development arose during Khrushchev's visit to London in the spring of 1955, when he teased the British Admiralty by predicting the end of naval forces, given 'missiles that can strike their targets from great distances'.[4] In conversation with Prime Minister Eden's wife Khrushchev defended Soviet missiles targeted on London and stated that the Soviet Union 'wouldn't tolerate being talked to in the language of ultimatums'.[5] The warning was clear and the launch of Sputnik on 4th October 1957 offered a checkmate to the United States as it demonstrated that the Soviet Union had mastered rocket technology and possessed intercontinental ballistic missiles. The security of the United States was immediately compromised as the warning time of a missile attack was only thirty minutes compared to two and a half hours for a conventional bomber attack.

The advantage to the Soviet Union was considerable as there was no defence against an attack from space and it was also a major propaganda triumph for Soviet technology at a time of the world-wide promotion of communism. Khrushchev hoped the 'missiles would force the West to treat the USSR with respect'[6] but the perception in the

United States was of an offensive capability rather than any Soviet attempt at security or equality. There was a rush to build nuclear-bomb shelters and fear of an imminent nuclear attack that would kill an estimated 50 million Americans. President Eisenhower was accused of complacency and in November 1957 the leaking of the CIA Gaither Report to the press deepened the American sense of doom. The Gaither Report confirmed a Soviet missile lead and predicted a 'missile gap' of 100 Soviet ICBMs to only 30 for the United States. A defence budget of 44 billion dollars over five years was recommended to close the gap and to construct civilian fallout shelters. The American sense of vulnerability was not helped when on live television, on 7th December 1957, a Vanguard rocket rose a mere two feet off the launch pad before exploding.

However, the reality of the Soviet threat was very different. The Soviet Union faced enormous technical difficulties in perfecting nuclear warheads and the mass production of rocket components and by 1959 had only deployed an estimated ten SS6 ICBMs. Nevertheless, in May 1959 Khrushchev placed his faith in missiles and designated the Soviet Strategic Rocket Force as a new branch of the Soviet armed forces. Khrushchev's commitment to missile forces was paid for by reductions in conventional forces, much to the annoyance of some members of the Politburo who measured success by clear gains for the Soviet Union.

Eisenhower refused to be panicked as U2 intelligence indicated a low deployment of Soviet ICBMs and he had confidence in the supremacy of SAC and the B52 bomber force. However, in an acceptance of some aspects of Soviet propaganda, Eisenhower did identify an 'education gap' and passed the Defense Education Act in 1958 which allocated 2 billion dollars to increase the teaching of science and technology in American universities.

President Kennedy inherited the sense of national insecurity in 1960, and after the failure of the Vienna Summit of June 1961 and the Berlin Wall confrontation of August 1961, he authorised a major review and increase in US conventional forces. Kennedy also acted to close the missile gap and authorised the deployment of 1054 Minuteman ICBMs and the construction of 41 nuclear submarines armed with Polaris missiles. The confidence of the United States was also restored by Kennedy's commitment in January 1961 to place a man on the moon by the end of the decade, and the subsequent success of the Mercury and Apollo space flights.

The Soviet lead and the missile gap proved to be a gross over-estimation and by the time of the Cuban Missile Crisis in October 1962 it was estimated that the United States had 4000 missile warheads targeted on the Soviet Union compared to 220 Soviet warheads targeted on the United States.

The unlimited budget of the United States had overwhelmed the Soviet Union but Khrushchev's strategy had succeeded in delivering the means to destroy the United States. In his memoirs Khrushchev records that Kennedy, in discussing the missile balance, stated that the Soviet Union only had enough missiles to 'wipe out the United States once'. Khrushchev had commented, 'once is quite enough'.[7] The missile race had conferred a parity of nuclear threat, and in recognition of this Kennedy abandoned the doctrine of 'massive retaliation' in favour of 'flexible response', which moved away from the first use of nuclear weapons. The joint deployment of nuclear submarines and construction of hardened missile silos also guaranteed a second-strike capability that forced both superpowers to accept that a future war would be a case of Mutually Assured Destruction (MAD).

In essence the Soviet Union had gained the dubious advantage of Mutually Assured Destruction but the disadvantage of a United States that developed an unassailable lead in the missile and space races.

Questions

1. Why did the Baruch Plan fail?
2. To what extent was Sputnik more propaganda than threat?

ANALYSIS (2): WHY DID THE CUBAN MISSILE CRISIS OCCUR? HOW FAR WAS THE RESOLUTION OF THE CRISIS A QUESTION OF MUTUAL COMPROMISE?

The island of Cuba presented the Soviet Union with a missile platform only ninety miles off the Florida coast and an opportunity to undermine the United States' overwhelming superiority in the missile race. It was an advantage Khrushchev could not ignore but the resulting crisis took the world to the brink of war in a tense confrontation that threatened to precipitate Armageddon.

President Kennedy gave his inaugural speech as president of the United States on 20th January 1961 and expressed the wish to slow down the missile race and to 'begin anew the quest for peace' but crucially he also gave the prophetic warning: 'let every other power know that this hemisphere intends to remain the master of its own house'.[8]

Kennedy was referring to the mounting crisis over Cuba that began on New Year's Day 1959 when Fidel Castro, after a long guerrilla campaign from 1952 to 1959, successfully overthrew the dictatorship of General Batista. Castro earned the enmity of the United States by initiating a social revolution that included the nationalisation of land owned by US companies without compensation. The United States tried and failed to moderate Castro's polices by refusing economic assistance, and in response Castro welcomed and accepted offers of Soviet economic aid in February 1960. This direct involvement of the Soviet Union in a Caribbean state was an immediate challenge to the United States as it transgressed the unspoken 'spheres of influence' that governed Cold War relations. The determination of the United States to oppose any communist penetration of the Western hemisphere had been demonstrated by the US intervention in Guatemala in June 1954. The State Department defended the intervention by stating, 'the master plan of international communism is to gain a solid political base in this hemisphere, a base that can be used to extend communist penetration'.[9] Here was an early warning that the spread of communism to any American state would be strongly opposed. Kennedy was determined to be seen to be defending the interests of the United States against the renewed Soviet challenge in Berlin and the Soviet presence in Cuba, which represented the extension of communism beyond Europe and Asia.

However, Kennedy made a significant mistake when he approved a CIA plan initiated by Eisenhower to train and arm a force of Cuban exiles to retake Cuba. It was an attractive proposition but the lightly armed force of 1400 men was easily outgunned and defeated by the Cuban Air Force and Army when they landed on the beaches of the Bay of Pigs on 17th April 1961. The incident was significant for two reasons. First, it indicated how strongly the United States opposed the Soviet penetration of Cuba. Second, it precipitated a military build-up on Cuba by driving Castro into an defensive alliance with the Soviet Union. The United States was subsequently forced to accept the flow of modern Soviet weapons and military advisers to Cuba as the price of the Bay of Pigs blunder.

By March 1962 there was a significant Soviet military presence on Cuba that was closely monitored by regular US U2 surveillance flights. The arrival of MiG jets and the installation of a surface-to-air (SAM) missile battery maintained a defensive posture but Kennedy was alert to the danger and in September 1962 warned the Soviet Union that the United States would not tolerate offensive weapons on Cuba. The United States was not concerned over the nuclear balance, which remained sharply in its favour, but was fearful of the Soviet Union gaining a devastating first-strike capability. A missile strike from Cuba would have reduced the warning time of a nuclear attack from thirty to two minutes and, in Sorensen's view, 'would have increased the temptation to launch a pre-emptive first strike'.[10] Consequently, the Soviet decision to place intermediate range ballistic missiles (IRBMs) on Cuba was a highly provocative act and bound to result in a major US response. Castro and Khrushchev gave contradictory explanations for the decision. Khrushchev informed the Supreme Soviet in December 1962 that Castro had requested nuclear weapons to deter a future US invasion whereas Castro stated in March 1963 that the initial proposal was made by Khrushchev. The genesis of the plan emerged during Khushchev's visit to Bulgaria in May 1962. While standing on the shores of the Black Sea, Defence Minister Malinovsky indicated the closeness of the US Jupiter missiles based in Turkey and Khrushchev immediately responded with the question, 'Can we not have bases close to America?'[11] Khrushchev confirmed this basic reasoning in his memoirs when he directly referred to the American military bases in Italy and Turkey and stated, 'it was high time America learned what it feels like to have her own land and her own people threatened'.[12] Khrushchev obviously hoped to seize a propaganda advantage after the humiliation of the Berlin Wall in August 1961 and to acquire a bargaining chip against the stationing of US nuclear missiles in Europe. It was a policy of risk but the prize would be a boost to Soviet prestige and a renewed advantage in the missile race.

The crisis broke on Monday, 15th October 1962, when photographs taken by a U2 spy plane over Cuba twenty-four hours earlier showed the construction of twenty-four missile pads for an estimated sixty-four IRBMs. President Kennedy was informed at 8.45 a.m. on 16th October and immediately assembled a crisis management team, the Executive Committee, to combat what was treated from the outset as an intolerable threat to the security of the United States. The immediate analysis was that Khrushchev would seek to reopen negotiations over Berlin and force a Western withdrawal. The military and political options were debated in secret within the White House. The chairman of the Joint Chiefs of Staff, General Taylor, recommended a 'surgical air strike' but it was to Kennedy's credit that he decided to seek a diplomatic solution. Kennedy made the crisis public in a live television broadcast at 7 p.m. on 22nd October, and so began one of the most tense weeks in the Cold War when a world-wide US military alert seemed to herald imminent war and possibly a nuclear exchange. There was criticism from some European allies, whom Sorensen acknowledged 'had long accustomed themselves to living next door to Soviet missiles'.[13] But the issue went beyond US security to the danger of Cuba becoming the much feared base for the communist penetration of the American states and a check to the US nuclear umbrella that protected the Western world. Kennedy's strategy was to place Cuba under 'quarantine' to prevent the delivery of any nuclear missiles to the island, but it has since been accepted that the CIA intelligence was flawed and that some nuclear warheads were already in place, including short-range, tactical weapons to be used purely to counter any US invasion. The attraction of the quarantine was that it gave time for diplomacy to take effect. Kennedy demonstrated his desire for a diplomatic solution by moving the quarantine 'trip line' around Cuba back to 500 miles from 800 miles to allow more time before the first Soviet ships were confronted by the US Navy.

Khrushchev, after the initial shock of discovery and the speed of the US reaction, insisted on 23rd October that the Soviet missiles were for defence, and in a letter to Bertrand Russell of 24th October invited the United States to participate in a summit.

The 'official' account of the crisis provided by Robert Kennedy in his book on the crisis, *Thirteen Days*, was of a resolute President Kennedy determined not to bargain or to compromise with the Soviet Union. However, in 1987 the White House aide Theodore Sorensen, who edited Robert Kennedy's manuscript for publication, admitted that he deleted references to the president's willingness to strike a deal. President Kennedy did offer to remove the US Jupiter missiles from Turkey and guaranteed not to invade Cuba in exchange for the complete removal of any nuclear weapons, including nuclear-capable aircraft, from Cuba. This was corroborated by the Soviet Union's ambassador Anatoly Dobrynin, who confirmed that the deal was discussed with Robert Kennedy. In 1994 Soviet archives provided evidence of the White House quid pro quo in a telegram from Dobrynin to the Kremlin dated 27th October 1962.

Kennedy did not pursue Khrushchev's offer of a summit as he had no wish to become trapped into long negotiations that would have given the Soviet Union a propaganda victory. Kennedy was willing to offer Khrushchev some concessions but he remained adamant that the missiles had to be withdrawn. There was never any question of a compromise that would have allowed the missiles to remain on Cuba. This robust stance reflected the US military assessment that any Soviet missiles on Cuba could be operational within ten days, after which time the security of the United States would be undermined.

Khrushchev found himself locked into a maelstrom of his own making and in an acknowledgement that 'the Americans were ready to fight'[14] he indicated by letter on 26th October that the missiles would be withdrawn. Apart from insisting upon an assurance that Cuba would not be invaded, the letter was conciliatory in tone but the following day Moscow radio and a second letter adopted a more hostile tone and raised demands for the removal of US missiles from Turkey. It would appear that the Politburo was anxious to secure more open concessions but Robert Kennedy proposed the strategy of ignoring the second letter and agreeing to the first. At 9 a.m. on 28th October Moscow radio broadcast that the crisis was over and in confirmation by letter Khrushchev agreed to remove the missiles under UN verification.

It was a significant US victory, summed up by Secretary of State Dean Rusk who stated, 'we were eyeball to eyeball and the other fellow just blinked'.[15] However, Kennedy was careful to play down the extent of the Soviet capitulation and ordered, 'no boasting, no gloating not even a claim of victory'.[16] He was sensitive not to humiliate the Soviet Union, and later in 1963, with minimal publicity, the US Jupiter missiles were removed from Turkey.

Khrushchev had to contend with an angry Castro who had expected the removal of the US military base at Guantanamo Bay to form part of any overall settlement.

Khrushchev, however, defended the outcome as a success and highlighted the United States' commitment not to invade Cuba as a worthy achievement that 'guaranteed the existence of a Socialist Cuba . . . a spectacular success without having to fire a single shot'.[17]

Within two years both leaders were gone. Kennedy was a victim of assassination on 22nd November 1963, and Khrushchev was forced into retirement in October 1964 by a Politburo critical of endless initiatives but few gains. Khrushchev's flamboyant boast that the Soviet Union could not only match but outperform the United States was silenced by the reality of the US lead in the missile race and the Soviet climbdown over Cuba.

The lasting compromise of Cuba was the mutual recognition that the missile race had taken both superpowers to the brink of war and that some arms limitation and detente was essential to govern future relations.

Questions

1. How justified was the United States' refusal to compromise over the stationing of nuclear missiles on Cuba?

2. Assess the relative importance of Khrushchev's motives: (a) the defence of Cuba? (b) an advantage in the missile race? (c) a bargaining chip over Berlin? (d) a bargaining chip over US missiles in Europe? (e) expansion of communism? (f) other?

SOURCES

1. THE MISSILE BALANCE

Source A: Sputnik.

Dr Blagonravov, a Soviet rocket scientist, interviewed on American television on 6th October 1957.

The Russian ambition, he declared, was to contribute to science and not to gain control over the Earth, and nobody should have anything to fear 'from the Soviet satellite programme'.

Source B: Eisenhower's statement on Sputnik.

President Eisenhower's statement on American television, 13th October 1957.

The Soviet launching of Earth satellites is an achievement of the first importance ... but in the main the Soviets continue to concentrate on the development of war-making weapons ... This, as well as their political attitude in international affairs, serves to warn us that Soviet expansionist aims have not changed.

Source C: NATO deployment of IRBMs.

Keesing Contemporary Archives, January 1961 record of NATO deployment of IRBMs.

The US Defense Department announced on 30th October 1959 that the number of Thor Intermediate Range Ballistic Missiles to be supplied to European allies had been reduced from five to four and that the Turkish government had agreed to establish one Jupiter IRBM squadron on its territory ... As a result there would be seven IRBM squadrons in Europe, two of Jupiter in Italy, one Jupiter in Turkey and four Thor in Britain.

Source D: the nuclear triad.

Strategic bombers

	1956	1960	1965	1970	1975	1979
United States	560	550	630	405	330	316
Soviet Union	60	175	200	190	140	140

ICBM

	1960	1964	1966	1968	1970	1972	1974	1979
United States	295	835	900	1054	1054	1054	1054	1054
Soviet Union	75	200	300	800	1300	1577	1587	1398

SLBM

	1962	1965	1968	1972	1975	1979
United States	145	500	656	656	656	656
Soviet Union	45	125	130	497	740	989

Questions

1. What is the unspoken fear contained in Source A?
*2. How do Sources A and B differ in their interpretation of Sputnik?
3. How far does the evidence of Source C support Soviet claims of a US nuclear advantage?
4. In light of the overall military balance in Europe how might NATO have justified the deployment of IRBMs?
5. Eisenhower placed his faith in the USAF strategic bomber force. How significant was the US lead from the evidence of Source D?
6. Considering all of the above four sources and your own knowledge, comment on how far the Soviet advantage in the missile race was an illusion.

Worked answer

*2. Source A emphasises the scientific importance of Sputnik and refers to the 'satellite programme' but it does not directly address the fact that Sputnik represents the Soviet acquisition of advanced rocket technology and an ICBM capability. The military application is implied in the words, 'nobody should have anything to fear', but the overall thrust of the statement is to reassure and emphasise the peaceful applications of the technology. In contrast it is the military applications that occupy Eisenhower in Source B. Whereas Eisenhower welcomes the advance in satellite technology as 'an achievement of the first importance', he castigates the Soviet Union for a focus on 'war-making weapons'. Eisenhower clearly mistrusts Soviet intentions and regards the development of rocket technology as a threat and a part of 'Soviet expansionist aims'. Consequently the sources differ in their interpretation of the intentions of the Soviet Union and the applications of the new rocket technology.

SOURCES

2. CUBAN MISSILE CRISIS: A WEEK IN *THE TIMES*

Source E: 22nd October 1962.

President Kennedy abruptly concluded his campaign tour at Chicago yesterday and returned to the capital. Mr Pierre Salinger, the White House Press Secretary, said that he had a slight cold, a condition that was not apparent to those who had accompanied him . . . There can be little doubt that something is going on.

Source F: 23rd October 1962.

'It shall be the policy of this nation,' Mr Kennedy said, 'to regard any nuclear missile strike launched from Cuba against any nation in the Western Hemisphere as an attack by the Soviet Union on the United States requiring a full retaliatory response upon the Soviet Union.'

Source G: 24th October 1962.

Russia today stopped all leave for the armed forces . . . The Soviet Government called America's intended actions towards Cuba an unheard of violation of international law.

Source H: 25th October 1962.

The American objective is to remove the missiles from Cuba . . . reference to the American missiles in Italy and Turkey was received with small enthusiasm.

Source I: 26th October 1962.

Both President Kennedy and Mr Khrushchev replied in conciliatory terms last night to the appeal by U Thant, Acting Secretary General of the United Nations, for two or three weeks' suspension of arms shipments to Cuba and of steps to search ships.

Source J: 27th October 1962.

The Cuban crisis worsened tonight with an announcement from the White House that the development of Soviet ballistic missile sites on the island was continuing at a rapid pace and apparently with the objective of achieving a full operational capacity as soon as possible. A direct military intervention cannot be ruled out . . . A military force with sufficient ships and aircraft is now poised in Florida for any action that the President may order.

Source K: 28th October 1962.

Mr Khrushchev agreed today to dismantle offensive missile bases in Cuba under United Nations verification, a decision which President Kennedy at once greeted as statesmanlike and a constructive contribution to peace.

Questions

1. Identify the evidence from *The Times* extracts that indicates that this was a significant crisis?
2. What possible solutions to the crisis are indicated by Sources H and I?
3. Comment on President Kennedy's attitude and response to the crisis as indicated by Sources F, H, J and K.
*4. How useful to the historian are newspaper accounts?
5. Considering all four sources and using your own knowledge, answer the following question: How effective were the strategies employed by President Kennedy to resolve the Cuban Missile Crisis?

Worked answer

*4. Newspaper accounts are an excellent primary source of information as they are written at the time of an event and often reflect the public mood and opinions. This is a valuable insight to the historian to balance against official accounts but newspapers also have significant weaknesses that have to be taken into account. It is important to identify the nation of origin of a particular newspaper, any declared political affiliations, the main readership and whether broadsheet or tabloid. A tabloid may adopt a more populist, sensationalist approach whereas a broadsheet is more likely to give a detailed analysis and indicate wider opinion. The possible bias of individual reporters is also an important consideration in terms of which facts and opinions are emphasised and which might be downplayed or ignored.

Consequently, newspaper accounts by themselves can never be accepted as a fully accurate source of history, but once balanced with other sources they are an invaluable aid to the historian in judging the importance and impact of a particular event.

5

DÉTENTE

BACKGROUND NARRATIVE

Both the United States and the Soviet Union were shaken by the Cuban Missile Crisis, which took the world to the brink of nuclear war. The mood was for détente and safeguards to limit the escalating nuclear arms race. The immediate result was the provision of a 'hotline' between Washington and Moscow, set up June 1963, and, in August of the same year, the Test Ban Treaty, which restricted the testing of nuclear weapons.

The Cuban Missile Crisis also had European repercussions as both France and Germany entered into independent diplomacy with the Soviet Union. France established trade relations with the Soviet Union in 1964 and withdrew all French forces from NATO in 1966. West Germany, under the leadership of Chancellor Willy Brandt, introduced the policy of Ostpolitik (Eastern Policy) from 1966 to 1972 and achieved a diplomatic breakthrough in relations with Eastern Europe.

The high point of détente was the 'triangular diplomacy' conducted by President Nixon and his foreign affairs adviser Henry Kissinger from 1971 to 1974. The People's Republic of China was admitted to the United Nations in October 1971, ending twenty-two years of isolation, and in February 1972 President Nixon travelled to Beijing for a summit meeting with Mao Zedong. The Soviet Union also entered into a series of summit meetings with the United States, and the result was trade agreements, arms limitations and a significant reduction in Cold War tension.

However, after the resignation of President Nixon in August

1974, as a result of the Watergate scandal, a chill began to return to the Cold War. Both President Ford (1974–77) and President Carter (1977–81) found it difficult to maintain détente against criticism of the Soviet Union's continued interventions in the Third World and breaches of the human rights provision of the Helsinki Accords of 1975. The fall of Saigon in April 1975 was also a humiliating debacle for the United States and soured the spirit of co-operation.

Finally, the Soviet invasion of Afghanistan in December 1979 reawakened fears of Soviet expansionism and marked the end of détente and the onset of a new Cold War.

ANALYSIS (1): HOW SUCCESSFULLY DID DÉTENTE INTRODUCE A NEW ERA INTO SUPERPOWER RELATIONS?

In many respects détente was a natural outcome of changes to the global balance of power. In 1967 the People's Republic of China (PRC) perfected the H-bomb and in 1969 the Soviet Union finally achieved nuclear parity with the United States. The result was 'triangular' diplomacy as the United States entered into a new era of co-operation rather than confrontation with the PRC and the Soviet Union.

The first indication of a shift in American thinking was provided by President Kennedy's speech to the American University in June 1963 only days before the first 'hotline' was installed between Washington and Moscow. Kennedy acknowledged the suffering and losses of the Soviet Union in the Second World War, hailed Soviet successes in science and industry and, in an echo of Khrushchev's policy of peaceful coexistence, stated, 'our most basic common link is that we all inhabit this small planet'.[1] The subsequent Nuclear Test Ban Treaty of August 1963 indicated the willingness of both Kennedy and Khrushchev to slow down the arms race, but this first flowering of détente was cut short by Kennedy's assassination on 22nd November 1963.

Within minutes of Kennedy's death, Vice-President Lyndon B. Johnson was sworn in as president of the United States onboard Air Force One at Dallas Airport, Texas. Less than a year later the leadership of the Soviet Union also changed when Khrushchev was ousted in the Politburo coup of October 1964, to be replaced by Leonid Brezhnev. The renewed attempts at détente were unsuccessful. Johnson met Soviet premier Kosygin at Glasborough, New Jersey, in July 1967, but differences over the Vietnam War prevented any meaningful dialogue, and after the Soviet invasion of Czechoslovakia in August 1968 Johnson cancelled a summit scheduled for October 1968. The only encouraging sign was the Nuclear Non-proliferation Treaty of 1968, which restricted nuclear technology to the five nuclear weapons states: the United States, the Soviet Union, China, France and Great Britain.

President Johnson's focus was Vietnam and his determination not to be the 'the President who saw Southeast Asia go the way China went'.[2] Johnson was a firm believer in Eisenhower's Domino Theory and in 1964 he committed US ground forces to Vietnam in a vigorous prosecution of the Vietnam War. It took a new president to accept that the Vietnam War was unwinnable.

Richard Nixon won the presidential elections of November 1968 with impeccable credentials as a Cold War warrior. However, his inaugural address in January 1969 demonstrated that his primary aim was détente. Nixon quoted Isaiah 2.4 from his family Bible: 'they shall beat their swords into plowshares', and further remarked that the greatest honour history can bestow 'is the title peacemaker'.[3] This was matched on the same day by an invitation from General Secretary Brezhnev for early discussions on arms limitations. Nixon appointed Henry Kissinger as his adviser on National Security Affairs and ignored the State Department in favour of secret diplomacy controlled directly from the Oval Office. The new style and the quest for détente was immediately in evidence. The Soviet ambassador, Anatoly Dobrynin, was invited to the White House on 17th February 1969, and thereafter attended regular lunch meetings with Nixon and Kissinger, using a private entrance to avoid press attention. This 'back channel' became a regular informal means of arriving at agreements outside of the formal state machinery.

Nixon confirmed a new direction in US foreign policy at a press conference on Guam in July 1969 while on a tour of the Pacific. The Nixon Doctrine essentially endorsed peaceful coexistence as the basis of superpower relations and abandoned the Truman Doctrine with its open-ended commitment to defend freedom around the world. The high human and matériel costs of the Korean and Vietnam wars had forced a reappraisal of where and if American forces would be committed to the defence of freedom. The test, according to Nixon, was if intervention was 'required by our own vital interests'.[4] The impact of the new doctrine was soon evident in Vietnam as the introduction of a Vietnamisation policy reduced the number of US ground troops from 480,000 in 1967 to 23,000 by 1973. However, Nixon's image as a 'peacemaker' was dented by his decision to substitute air power for ground power in a vain attempt to bomb the Viet Cong into submission.

It only served to extend the war into neutral Cambodia and provoke mass protest in the United States and Europe.

Nixon's conversion to détente was also a recognition that the United States no longer possessed overwhelming nuclear superiority. It was estimated that the Soviet Union had quadrupled its ICBM force since the time of the Cuban Missile Crisis in 1962. Mutually Assured Destruction was the uncomfortable reality of any future war and both sides, after the shock of Cuba, were keen to establish rules of engagement and, in Kissinger's words, 'to limit the risks of nuclear conflict'.[5]

The perception of a communist monolith was also dispelled by open confrontation between the Soviet Union and the PRC that erupted into the border fighting along the Ussuri River in March 1969. The fact that the Soviet Union stationed twenty-five divisions along the Sino-Soviet border compared to only twelve divisions in Europe spoke volumes. In September 1969 Nixon played the 'China card' by criticising the Soviet Union for its provocative build up of troops on the border. The United States found itself in the advantageous position of being courted by both governments as neither wished to be isolated in a two-against-one realignment. Kissinger became the arch exponent of this 'triangular diplomacy' and in later years 'shuttle diplomacy', as he travelled the Third World and used his considerable persuasive powers to broker agreements. The Nixon Doctrine returned the world to the familiar politics of 'national interest' and ended the sterile trench warfare of ideological opposition. The Cold War became grey rather than black and white.

The transition in US policy was dramatically illustrated by the diplomatic recognition of the People's Republic of China after decades of bitter animosity over Communist China's involvement in the Korean and Vietnam wars. The first indications of change arose in 1969 with the easing of travel and trade restrictions with the PRC, followed in April 1971 by 'Ping Pong' diplomacy when an American table-tennis team visited the PRC. Cautious hints at co-operation were exchanged by both sides, and in July 1971 Kissinger, under the cover of a visit to Pakistan, embarked on Operation Polo and flew secretly to Beijing to explore rapprochement. The first result of the new accord was the PRC's admittance to the United Nations in October 1971 in place of the Nationalist government based in Taiwan. The United States had stubbornly defended the Chinese Nationalists as the legitimate government of China ever since they were defeated in the Chinese Civil War of 1946–49 and fled to Taiwan. On 17th February 1972 Nixon flew to Beijing and was received at the airport by Prime Minister Zhou Enlai. In a piece of political theatre Nixon insisted upon descending the steps of

Air Force One alone to shake hands warmly with the premier. This corrected the insult when, at the height of the Cold War, Secretary of State Dulles had refused to shake hands with Zhou Enlai. The summit ended with the Shanghai Communiqué and was according to Nixon, 'the week that changed the world'.[6] The communiqué included a joint declaration that neither side wished hegemony over the Pacific region and in a pointed reference to the Soviet Union declared that both powers would resist any such intention by a third power. In return for this open check to the Soviet Union the PRC ended its ritual denunciation of the United States as the capitalist enemy. Realpolitik on both sides had replaced the ideological straitjackets that had governed relations in the 1950s.

The Soviet Union attempted to engage the United States in a summit before Nixon's visit to the PRC, in a clear indication of Soviet fears of Chinese intentions. Brezhnev even played down the loss of two Soviet ships to US mines along the Vietnamese coastline. The Soviet Union was concerned by a mounting ideological and military challenge from the PRC, particularly after 1971 with the arrival of a PRC voice in the United Nations. The PRC condemned the Soviet invasion of Czechoslovakia in August 1968 and the Brezhnev Doctrine of November 1968 as examples of Soviet imperialism. In July the state visit of President Ceauşescu of Romania to Beijing provided further evidence of the PRC encouraging communist states to look east for leadership. The leadership of the communist world was in open contention.

President Nixon travelled to Moscow in May 1972 for a summit that focused upon arms control. In was in the interests of both superpowers to control the spiralling costs of the nuclear arms race. The result was a Strategic Arms Limitation Treaty (SALT) that fixed the numbers of ICBMs held by both sides and an Anti-Ballistic Missile (ABM) Treaty that restricted deployment of ABM systems. There were also a number of wider agreements on health, environmental concerns and trade deals, including the first Soviet Pepsi Cola plant. The Soviet Union also negotiated a wheat deal in October 1972, which was so extensive and at such favourable rates that it was referred to as the 'great grain robbery'. The overall value of US–Soviet trade leapt upwards from 67 million dollars in 1971 to 490 million dollars by 1973. Nixon's inaugural statement that 'after a period of confrontation we are entering an era of negotiation'[7] was shown to be a firm reality as détente substantially improved US relations with the Soviet Union and the PRC. Détente also boosted Nixon's appeal on the re-election trail and he was returned as president with a landslide majority in November 1972. A summit in

Washington 1973 and a return to Moscow in 1974 marked the high points of détente, and a flurry of agreements allowed Nixon to boast that more had been achieved in two years than in the first twenty years of the Cold War.

Nixon's only failure was in establishing a policy of 'linkage' and 'seeking Soviet concessions in other areas as the price for American participation in SALT'.[8] Uppermost in Nixon's mind was to achieve an honourable withdrawal from Vietnam as negotiations with North Vietnam entered the final phase in 1973–75. There was also considerable US concern over Soviet support for Egypt and Arab nations against Israel in the Yom Kippur War of October 1973. The war invoked the first use of the 'hotline' and a world-wide US military alert. Brezhnev rejected all attempts at 'linkage' and also sacked the hard-liner Pyotr Shelest from the Politburo in 1973 after he sought to encourage a measure of Soviet 'linkage' against US policy in Vietnam. Brezhnev was determined to keep détente separate from the wider promotion of communism. Like Khrushchev before him, he believed in the eventual victory of world communism. Consequently, the Third World was treated as a legitimate area of superpower competition for client states and was entirely separate from arms control.

In August 1974 détente stumbled after President Nixon was forced to resign over the Watergate scandal. The Soviet chief foreign affairs adviser to the Kremlin, Georgi Arbatov, later praised Nixon for establishing 'a new more realistic American role in the world'.[9] Consequently, it was President Ford who met Brezhnev at Vladivostok in November 1974 to pursue SALT, but support for détente in the United States was on the wane, eroded by criticism of Soviet restrictions on Jewish emigration to Israel. A hostile Congress Bill, the Jackson–Vanik Amendment of January 1975, cut trade with the Soviet Union in a determined effort to secure 'linkage' to Jewish emigration rights. Relations were further harmed by the Soviet and Cuban intervention in the Angolan civil war of 1975 and later interventions in Mozambique, Somalia and Ethiopia which, to Western opinion, conflicted with the spirit of détente. The fall of Saigon in April 1975 and the overall victory of communism in Vietnam was also a bitter moment for the United States and created a climate of opposition to any further concessions to the Soviet Union. Finally, the rise of internal dissent in the Soviet Union added significantly to the hardening of Western opinion as it focused attention on Soviet human rights abuses that conflicted with the Helsinki Accords of 1975. The Soviet dissidents Andrey Sakharov and Alexander Solzhenitsyn were fêted in Western capitals as symbols of Soviet injustice and both encouraged pressure to be placed on the

Soviet Union to adhere to the provisions of the Helsinki Accords. The anti-Soviet mood was so pronounced by 1976 that President Ford ordered the word détente to be struck from all of his presidential election speeches and literature.

Effectively, détente with the Soviet Union was over. Jimmy Carter was elected president in November 1976 and provoked Soviet objections by trying to link détente to verifiable progress in human rights. Secretary of State Kissinger retired in 1977 and was replaced by Cyrus Vance and the magic was lost. Brezhnev clashed with Vance over his open publication of the terms for a SALT II Treaty, a tactic that struck Brezhnev as a dictat. SALT II was eventually signed by Brezhnev and Carter at the Vienna Summit of June 1979 but the relationship was distinctly cool. By contrast, relations with the People's Republic of China continued to improve and most favoured nation status was granted in January 1980. The fact that there was no strategic missile threat from the PRC allowed for a closer US relationship and the rapid blossoming of peaceful coexistence.

The death knell of détente with the Soviet Union was finally sounded by the Soviet invasion of Afghanistan in December 1979, which rekindled the dormant fears of Soviet expansionism. In protest President Carter scrapped the SALT II Treaty in January 1980, although in practice it was observed, and in July 1980 he promoted a boycott of the Moscow Olympic Games. However, Carter was castigated for weakness in failing to match the growth of the Soviet military forces and his inability to resolve the hostage crisis in Iran after the US embassy in Teheran was overrun by Islamic militants in November 1979. In this volatile atmosphere Ronald Reagan was elected president in November 1980, with a mandate for counter-action.

Détente collapsed in 1980 but it provided essential lubrication and reduced the friction in the transition from a bipolar to a triangular Cold War.

Questions

1. Identify and compare the aims of the United States, the People's Republic of China and the Soviet Union. How far did each nation achieve its aims?
2. To what extent did détente introduce a new era of co-operation?

ANALYSIS (2): IN WHAT WAYS WAS OSTPOLITIK A BREAK-THROUGH IN EUROPEAN RELATIONS?

The division of Germany was the focal point of the Cold War in Europe. Berlin, in particular, was the frozen front line and a potent flash point in 1948, 1958 and 1961. Ostpolitik promoted a thaw in German relations and created the first significant chinks in the Iron Curtain.

East Germany was an artificial creation, a product of the post-war confrontation, and with borders decided not by mutual dialogue and treaty but by the reach of the Red Army. The declaration of the German Federal Republic (GFR) in September 1949 and the German Democratic Republic (GDR) in October 1949 represented the failure of the occupying Four Powers (United States, Soviet Union, France and Great Britain) to agree the status of Germany rather than a planned act of nation-building. This was reflected in the constitution of the GFR, which laid a claim to the whole of Germany and the restoration of Germany's 1937 borders before they were distended by Hitler's policies of Grossdeutschland and *Lebensraum*. The determination of the GFR eventually to reunite Germany was evident in the Hallstein Doctrine of 1955, named after Foreign Minister Hallstein. The Hallstein Doctrine refused to recognise East Germany as a legitimate state and threatened to end diplomatic relations with any country that traded with the GDR. Yugoslavia fell foul of this ruling in 1957, as did Cuba in 1963. West Germany assumed that the Soviet Union would enter into negotiation and eventually agree to a reunited Germany. However, after the Berlin Wall was erected in August 1961, the focus of the Cold War switched to Vietnam and a new front line. The Cold War moved on, but to ordinary Germans the Wall was a permanent reminder of the division of their country.

It was the entry of France into independent détente with the Soviet Union in 1964–66 that opened up the possibilities for a dialogue in Europe separate from the world-wide superpower confrontation. Opinion in France and wider Europe was hostile to the US policy in the Vietnam War and the unilateral actions of the United States in the Cuban Missile Crisis, which might have involved NATO in a nuclear war. In 1960 France, with the assurance of an independent nuclear deterrent, attempted to reassert her past authority as a European power. To demonstrate independence, France gradually withdrew from NATO between 1959 and 1966 but was ultimately disappointed by the limited response of the Soviet Union, and in 1974 French forces returned to NATO.

France had little of significance to offer the Soviet Union beyond trade, but West Germany could offer a normalisation of relations and end the diplomatic isolation of East Germany. This was an attractive proposition for the Soviet Union and worthy of exploration. The initiative was taken by West Germany in March 1966 with the issue of a six-point Ostpolitik (Eastern policy) for the improvement of relations with Eastern Europe. Willy Brandt, the foreign minister of the GFR, secured agreement for the Ostpolitik proposals at a meeting of the Council of NATO Foreign Ministers in December 1966. During the West German election campaign of October 1966 Brandt was dogged by allegations that he was an active agent for the Soviet Union but the evidence arising from Swedish wartime files of Soviet sympathisers was dismissed as an election smear. In June 1998 the allegations were renewed, based on the testimony of a senior Soviet intelligence officer, but to date no firm documentary evidence has been presented to show that Ostpolitik was open to Soviet manipulation.

Brandt's initiative was motivated by the lack of superpower action to settle the issue of divided Germany. President Johnson angered German opinion in October 1966 by indicating that any change in Germany's status would be as a result of détente rather than a prerequisite of détente. In other words Germany was not high on the US agenda despite the Berlin Wall, which separated families and abandoned East Germans to the hardships imposed by a backward economy. Ordinary East Germans were not the enemy but fellow Germans enmeshed in superpower politics. The Wall was a visual reminder of the failure of superpower politics and a powerful prompt to the West German government for independent action.

The first tentative step in Ostpolitik was the recognition of Romania in January 1967, an act that immediately rescinded the Hallstein Doctrine. The states of Eastern Europe reacted with considerable caution and at the Karlovy Vary Conference in Czechoslovakia in April 1967 there was suspicion that Brandt's aim was to normalise relations with Eastern Europe state by state, with the exception of East Germany, which would be ignored and finally isolated. The first secretary of the GDR Communist Party, Walter Ulbricht, was also wary of any warming of relations that might ignite German nationalism. Brandt's commitment to Ostpolitik increased after December 1967, when NATO approved 'flexible response' as its revised European defence strategy. The strategy addressed the superiority of Warsaw Pact conventional forces in Europe and planned for the 'first use' of battlefield nuclear weapons by NATO in the event of an overwhelming advance by the Warsaw Pact. It made good military sense but as Germany was the most likely future battleground, 'flexible response' was an uncomfortable prospect for Brandt and Germany.

In February 1968 Brandt made a direct approach to the Soviet Union, but the Prague Spring of anti-Soviet protests and the subsequent Soviet invasion of Czechoslovakia in August 1968 disrupted the détente process. The Soviet Union accused Brandt of promoting unrest in Czechoslovakia by encouraging the states of Eastern Europe to adopt a more independent stance. Brandt was not deterred and in September 1968 he renewed his quest for better relations, by lifting the ban on the West German Communist Party. In January 1969 the Soviet Union finally responded by entering into direct talks. However, there was no immediate breakthrough as the Soviet Union harboured a fear of a powerful reunited Germany allied to NATO and ultimately German revanchism. The United States was also wary of independent German détente and 'feared for the unity of the West'.[10] However, the United States had little choice but to accept the initiative, as in October 1969 Willy Brandt was elected chancellor of the German Federal Republic. Brandt immediately calmed Soviet fears by denying any wish to undermine the GDR and offered a beneficial increase in trade relations and compensation for the victims of Nazism. Crucially, he also offered recognition of the Oder–Neisse Line that the Soviet Union had unilaterally defined in 1945 as the border of Poland deep inside German territory. The pre-war Polish corridor to the sea had expanded westwards into a deep wedge of German land that the GFR constitution of 1949 had pledged to restore to a united Germany. Brandt also ended a major Soviet nightmare in November 1969 when he signed the Nuclear Non-proliferation Treaty and renounced any prospect of the GFR gaining independent nuclear weapons. Brandt's foreign policy adviser Egon Bahr went further and proposed the creation of a demilitarised zone in Central Europe free from NATO or Warsaw Pact forces, but this was abandoned as unrealistic. Ostpolitik was irresistible to the Soviet Union and this in part explains the suspicions that Brandt was in collusion with the USSR. Regardless of the truth, Ostpolitik was a significant breakthrough in the Cold War as it offered a settlement of the vexed German question. Ulbricht, however, feared movement towards German unity on West Germany's terms and he demanded the unequivocal recognition of the GDR as an independent German state. Ulbricht's attitude was hardened by the rapturous reception given to Brandt's during two visits to the GDR in March and May 1970, as it indicated that the sympathies and loyalties of the East Germans were more West than East. Brandt looked to the Soviet Union for progress and in August 1970 signed a

Non-aggression Pact with the Soviet Union, thirty-one years after Hitler had concluded the Nazi–Soviet Pact with very different intentions. The treaty recognised the reality of a divided Germany but the benefits of mutual collaboration. In a further break with the past Brandt visited Poland in December 1970, and formally recognised Poland's new border along the Oder–Neisse Line. He also publicly renounced the past by kneeling in quiet contemplation in front of the monument to the Warsaw ghetto in an act of atonement for the scourge of Nazism. Ostpolitik was the hand of friendship across the Iron Curtain and in May 1971 Ulbricht was replaced as the first secretary of the GDR Communist Party by Erich Honecker in a move that signified a new beginning in East–West relations.

Berlin remained under the jurisdiction of the Four Powers but a Four Power conference in September 1971 endorsed Ostpolitik and authorised a relaxation of the border controls. Berliners gained improved two-way access and direct telephone lines, which eased the plight of divided families. In recognition of Brandt's success he was awarded the Nobel Peace Prize in October 1971. Brandt's Ostpolitik policy of 'two states but one nation' became a reality as the close ties between East and West Germany were confirmed, and this reality formed the basis of the 'Basic Treaty' between West Germany and the Soviet Union of December 1972. The Basic Treaty stopped short of recognising the GDR as a separate German state but permanent missions were established to promote the welfare of all of the German people in both the East and West. Kissinger remarked, 'Berlin disappeared from the list of international crisis spots'[11] and in May 1973 Brezhnev became the first Soviet leader to visit Bonn.

Ostpolitik was an historic compromise that ended the stark division of the post-war period and paved the way for the Mutual Balanced Force Reduction (MFBR) talks January 1973, which discussed limits to Warsaw Pact and NATO forces. The Soviet Union's desire for a European security conference to review and ratify European borders was also acknowledged and after preliminary talks all thirty-three European nations with the addition of Canada and the United States met in Helsinki in July 1975. Thirty years after Potsdam the Soviet occupation of Eastern Europe was recognised and the Soviet Union in response accepted 'linkage' to the Basket III provisions that guaranteed basic human rights for all European citizens. Later this became a significant factor in the collapse of détente as the Soviet Union found itself in regular breach of the Helsinki Accords. Helsinki became a 'Trojan Horse' as the peoples of Eastern Europe and especially Poland increasingly demanded more political freedom.

Helsinki confirmed the existence of East and West Germany but the reality of one German people was never in doubt and in 1989 the withdrawal of Soviet support for the GDR led to the immediate dismantlement of the Berlin Wall and a formal declaration of a reunited Germany on 12th September 1990. Ulbricht's suspicions were correct.

Ostpolitik significantly eased the Cold War tension in Europe and gave not just Germany but the whole of Europe hope for peaceful coexistence.

Questions

1. Why was the reunification of Germany such a contentious issue for the Soviet Union?
2. To what extent did the Four Powers fail Germany?

SOURCES

1. SUCCESS OF DÉTENTE

Source A: Kennedy's address to the American University.

On 10th June 1962 President Kennedy gave the following address to the American University.

No government or social system is so evil that its people must be considered as lacking in virtue. As Americans we find communism profoundly repugnant as a negation of personal freedom and dignity. But we can still hail the Russian people for their many achievements in science and space, in economic and industrial growth, in culture and in acts of courage ... In short, both the United States and its allies and the Soviet Union and its allies have a mutually deep interest in a just and genuine peace and in halting the arms race.

Source B: Nixon's State of the Nation address.

Extract from President Nixon's State of the Nation address, 20th January 1972.

I shall soon be visiting the People's Republic of China and the Soviet Union. I shall go there with no illusions. We have great differences with both powers. We will continue to have great differences. But peace depends on the ability of Great Powers to live together on the same planet despite their differences. We would not be true to our obligations to generations yet unborn if we failed to seize the moment to do everything in our power to ensure that we will be able to talk about these differences rather than fight about them.

Source C: the Shanghai Communiqué.

Extract from President Nixon's memoirs on the signing of the Shanghai Communiqué with the People's Republic of China, 27th February 1972.

There are essential differences between China and the United States in their social systems and foreign policies. However, the two sides agreed that countries, regardless of their social systems, should conduct their relations on the principles of respect for the sovereignty and territorial integrity of all states . . . both wish to reduce the danger of international military conflict; neither should seek hegemony in the Asia–Pacific region and each is opposed to efforts by any other country or group of countries to establish such hegemony.

Source D: aims of Soviet foreign policy.

The revised constitution of the Soviet Union, 7th October 1977, included the following statement of foreign policy aims.

The foreign policy of the USSR is aimed at ensuring international conditions favourable for building communism in the USSR, safeguarding the state interests of the Soviet Union, consolidating the positions of world socialism, supporting the struggle of peoples for national liberation and social progress, preventing wars of aggression, achieving universal and complete disarmament and consistently implementing the principle of the peaceful coexistence of states with different social systems.

Source E: Soviet intervention in the Third World.

Konstantin Chernenko, a future leader of the USSR, defended Soviet interventions in the Third World at the Twenty-fifth Congress of the CPSU, February 1976.

One of the fundamentals of the foreign policy of our Party and the Soviet state has been and will remain solidarity with the peoples who have shattered the fetters of colonial dependence and embarked on the path of independent development. Especially, of course, with peoples who have to repel the attacks of the aggressive forces of imperialism which is creating very dangerous seats of bloody violence and war conflagration in one part of the world after another . . . Our Party's stand on these issues is clear, pure and noble. And we will unswervingly adhere to it.

Source F: Brezhnev in the United States.

Extract from General Secretary Brezhnev's television broadcast to the American people, 24th June 1973.

Mankind has outgrown the rigid armour of the Cold War which it once had to wear. It wants to breathe freely and peacefully ... The historical path we have travelled has not been an easy one. Our people take great pride that in the short historical period since the victory of the socialist revolution a backward Russia has turned into a major industrial power and achieved outstanding successes in science and culture ... A year ago in Moscow we laid the foundations for improving Soviet–American relations. Now this great and important objective has been successfully brought closer. It is our hope that this trend will continue, for it meets the interests of our two great peoples and of all mankind.

Questions

*1. Define the phrase 'seek hegemony' in the context of Source C?

2. What compromise on the part of President Nixon is evident in Sources B and C?

3. How far is there agreement between President Kennedy (Source A), President Nixon (Source B) and General Secretary Brezhnev (Source F)?

4. In what ways do the Soviet constitution (Source D) and Chernenko (Source E) pose a challenge to the Western world?

5. Considering the evidence of Sources A to F and your own wider knowledge, answer the following question: Outline and evaluate the challenges and successes of President Nixon's 'triangular diplomacy'?

Worked answer

*1. In the context of Source C the phrase 'seek hegemony' appears as a joint pledge from the United States and the PRC that neither will attempt to impose their political or military leadership or hegemony upon the Asia–Pacific region. The declaration also warns other unspecified nations not to attempt hegemony or dominance of the region and to respect 'the sovereignty and territorial integrity of all states'.

SOURCES

2. CONSIDERING OSTPOLITIK

Source G: West German statement.

On 25th March 1966 the West German government issued a formal six-point statement seeking an improvement in relations with Eastern Europe.

The German people wish to live in peace and freedom. They consider it their greatest national task to remove the partition of Germany under which they have suffered for many years ... The German people desire to live on good terms with all, including their East German neighbours. Hence the Federal Government has been trying in various ways to improve relations with the states and peoples of Eastern Europe.

Source H: Soviet response to West Germany.

On 17th May 1966 the Soviet Union responded to the West German statement.

The GFR ranks second among the NATO countries after the United States in the level of military expenditure ... Hundreds of openly Nazi, militarist and revanchist organisations are active in the Federal Republic ... Citizens of the Federal Republic are being poisoned literally from childhood with the venom of militarist and revanchist ideas which also colour school syllabuses, literature, the press, films and television ... The frontier along the Oder and Neisse ... is final and unalterable.

Questions

1. Explain the 'partition' of Germany referred to in Source G?
2. Compare and contrast the differences in style and tone of Sources G and H?
3. Considering both Sources G and H and your own wider knowledge, answer the following question: Why was the future of Germany such a potent issue in East–West relations?

6

DISARMAMENT

BACKGROUND NARRATIVE

The United Nations Charter of 1945 predated the existence of nuclear weapons, but in 1952 the United Nations (UN) passed Resolution 502 which set the objective of the prohibition of all nuclear weapons. The resolution had little immediate impact as the race to perfect H-bomb technology from 1950 to 1954 prevented any meaningful dialogue between the nuclear weapons states.

The destructive force of the H-bomb horrified the world, and after the Berlin Crisis of August 1961 the United Nations established an Eighteen Nation Disarmament Committee (ENDC) to pursue disarmament. The ENDC was convened in Geneva in March 1962, but expectations were low. An arithmetically minded American journalist calculated that prior to the Geneva Conference there had been 863 international conferences on disarmament that between them generated a total of 17,000 hours of discussion, or approximately 18 million words, and all without agreement.

However, the Cuban Missile Crisis of October 1962 took the United States and the Soviet Union to the brink of nuclear war and convinced both superpowers of the need for limitations. The immediate disarmament successes were the Test Ban Treaty of 1963, the Outer Space Treaty of 1967 and the Nuclear Non-proliferation Treaty of 1968.

In 1969 the Soviet Union achieved nuclear parity with the United States and the certainty of Mutually Assured Destruction (MAD) and the emerging competition to develop anti-ballistic missiles (ABMs) and multiple independently targeted re-entry vehicles (MIRVs) encouraged both superpowers to pursue disarmament.

Détente and disarmament became two sides of the same coin in the 1970s as both superpowers engaged in direct Strategic Arms Limitation Talks (SALT), and in Europe NATO and the Warsaw Pact engaged in the Mutual Balanced Force Reduction Talks (MBFR). The United Nations declared the 1970s as the Decade of Disarmament but the talks were not a complete success. In 1979 the Soviet Union deployed SS20 nuclear missiles in Europe and NATO responded with plans for the deployment of cruise and Pershing II missiles. Disarmament finally collapsed in January 1980, with the withdrawal of the SALT II Treaty by President Carter in protest at the Soviet invasion of Afghanistan.

In November 1980 the election of President Reagan marked the renewal of the arms race, symbolised for a generation by the Strategic Defense Initiative (SDI) or, more popularly, Star Wars.

ANALYSIS (1): HOW COMMITTED WERE THE UNITED STATES AND THE SOVIET UNION TO DISARMAMENT?

The United Nations' Decade of Disarmament 1970–80 ended with the paradox of a substantial increase rather than a decrease in the number of nuclear warheads deployed. However, this apparent failure of disarmament belied a significant commitment to disarmament by both superpowers in a determined effort to end the arms race.

After the Cuban Missile Crisis of October 1962 the superpowers came under sustained UN and public pressure for nuclear disarmament. The Campaign for Nuclear Disarmament (CND), in particular, politicised a whole generation and raised public awareness of the consequences of a nuclear war. The subsequent passage of the Test Ban Treaty of 1963, the Outer Space Treaty of 1967 and the Nuclear Non-proliferation Treaty of 1968 gave hope for full disarmament.

Arms limitation was attractive to both superpowers not only to reduce the dangers of war but to curb the high financial costs of weapons development. Defence costs in 1969 were running at an estimated 39.7 billion dollars for the United States, approximately 7 per cent of national income, against an estimated 42 billion dollars for the Soviet Union, which was an estimated 15 per cent of the meagre Soviet national income. The development of the Soviet anti-ballistic missile (ABM) system 'Galosh' and the United States' equivalent 'Sentinel' system in 1967 also promised a new round of defence spending. In addition, both sides were developing multiple independently targeted re-entry vehicle (MIRV) technology that permitted a single missile to carry more than one nuclear warhead. At the Glasborough Summit of July 1967 President Johnson and Soviet Premier Kosygin agreed to explore joint limitations, but a conference scheduled for October 1968 was cancelled in protest at the Soviet invasion of Czechoslovakia.

President Nixon captured the public mood for disarmament in his inauguration address in January 1969 with an unambiguous commitment to peace and disarmament. Brezhnev simultaneously invited Nixon to participate in disarmament talks, and in November 1969 the first preliminary disarmament talks were convened in Helsinki. In advance Nixon had deliberately authorised the development of a revised ABM programme, 'Safeguard', in August 1969 as 'a bargaining chip with the Soviets'.[1] Nixon was determined to negotiate from a position of strength but his stated goal was nuclear 'sufficiency' rather than nuclear 'superiority'. Nixon wanted a defence strategy that offered options other than Mutually Assured Destruction. He also wanted the guarantee that the United States could survive a Soviet 'first strike' given improvements to missile guidance systems and deployment of the SS9 ICBM that carried an awesome 25-megaton warhead. The development of an ABM system offered a potent counter-force to the Soviet Strategic Rocket Force.

After a massive investment between 1964 and 1969 the Soviet Union had achieved nuclear parity with the United States, and by 1969 possessed an estimated 1198 ICBMs against 1054 ICBMs for the United States. The development of ABM systems threatened to lock both sides into a new defence race that the Soviet Union could ill afford. The outbreak of riots in Poland in 1970 against low wages and food shortages indicated the dangers of neglecting social improvements. The need for more consumer-orientated spending was later confirmed by Brezhnev in a television broadcast to the American people in 1973 when he stated, 'we want to effect a considerable rise in the living standards of the Soviet people'.[2]

Consequently, Nixon's ABM 'bargaining chip' commanded the attention of the Soviet Union, but in return for an ABM treaty the United States wanted a comprehensive SALT treaty to freeze the deployment of Soviet ICBMs. The talks were deadlocked throughout the 1970s as the Soviet Union resisted the linkage and because of the sheer technical complexity of defining and balancing weapons systems. The Soviet lead in ICBMs did not confer overall nuclear superiority, as in 1970 the United States possessed a lead in strategic bombers and submarines. The figure for 'launchers' (which counted the delivery systems of strategic bombers, submarines and ICBMs) gave the United

States an advantage of 2109 to an estimated 1431 for the Soviet Union. In total across the nuclear triad the United States deployed an estimated 4736 warheads against 1815 Soviet warheads. The different 'throw weights' or megatonnage of individual warheads and the application of MIRV technology added further confusion to a very complex set of negotiations.

President Nixon appealed directly to Brezhnev in January 1971 for progress and after some initial hesitation an agreement was reached to proceed with ABM and SALT treaties. Nixon announced the 'significant development in breaking the deadlock' on national television on 20th May 1971.[3] Both treaties were signed during the first Brezhnev–Nixon summit in Moscow in May 1972 after some late-night detailed discussions between Foreign Ministers Kissinger and Gromyko. The ABM Treaty restricted ABMs to the capital cities of Washington and Moscow and to one specified ICBM site in each country. The Interim Agreement (SALT I) set a five-year freeze on the numbers of ICBMs and SLBMs and, for reasons of verification simplicity, ignored MIRV technology. The agreement permitted an increase in the number of Soviet Union ICBMs from 1530 to 1610, against the United States' total of 1054 ICBMs, while SLBMs were fixed at 950 for the USSR and 710 for the United States. This difference took into account the US superiority in strategic aircraft and superiority in MIRV technology. By 1972 the further application of MIRV technology provided the United States with an estimated 7601 warheads to 2573 Soviet warheads. The US warheads were also spread across a wider mix of delivery systems that guaranteed a second-strike capability.

SALT I was not disarmament but the specification of a numerical base line of the strategic weapons possessed by both superpowers. This was an essential first step to facilitate future joint verifiable disarmament. Gromyko stated, 'in the history of international relations it is difficult to find another example of such fruitful results achieved through negotiation'.[4] Ten years after the Cuban Missile Crisis there was considerable hope for a peaceful future.

The confidence engendered by the ABM and SALT I treaties also produced the Biological Warfare Treaty of April 1972, which agreed the destruction of existing stockpiles and prohibited the development of future chemical or bacteriological weapons. This treaty was ratified by the United Nations in May 1972 and outlawed an entire class of offensive weapons.

Action was also taken to outlaw further platforms for nuclear weapons in the Seabed Treaty of 1971 and the Outer Space Treaty of 1967. Together with the Nuclear Non-proliferation Treaty of 1968, the spread and development of nuclear weapons was being corralled by international law and provided a firm base for future disarmament. In the opinion of Ambrose, 'for the first time in the Cold War there was a constituency for peace'.[5]

However, the constituency in the United States was fragile as the disarmament process came under increasing attack from a vocal Jewish lobby anxious to secure linkage to improvements in the emigration rights of Soviet Jews. The Pentagon was also critical of disarmament and concerned that too much was being conceded. Sufficient unrest was stirred within Congress to deny the Soviet Union most favoured nation trading status, much to Nixon's irritation.

Brezhnev arrived in Washington on 16th June 1973 for the second summit with Nixon but he also disappointed Nixon by requesting a delay to the SALT II Treaty. Brezhnev was fending off his own hawks in the Politburo who were insisting upon more time for the Soviet Union to match US MIRV technology before setting limits. The best Nixon could achieve was an Agreement on the Prevention of Nuclear War, by which both superpowers agreed not to take actions that might result in war. It was an affirmation of peaceful coexistence and, coupled with Brezhnev's very warm and open appeal for peace to the American people on national television during his visit, held out the prospect of future settlement.

The future of disarmament to a large extent depended upon the confidence and personal chemistry between Brezhnev and Nixon, and Kissinger and Gromyko. By the time of the third summit in Moscow in June 1974, Nixon was fatally flawed by the Watergate investigation and was facing proceedings for his impeachment. Nixon pressed Brezhnev for a SALT II treaty but, as Nixon noted in his memoirs, the Politburo and Pentagon hawks were blocking 'the real prospect of arms reduction'.[6] Opinion in the Pentagon as represented by Secretary of Defense Schlesinger was also firmly opposed to the SALT II proposal for a freeze on US warheads while the Soviet Union increased warheads to the US level. It appeared to the Pentagon that Nixon was giving away the US lead and endangering national security when all of the evidence of Soviet actions in the Third World pointed to aggressive expansion.

A SALT II treaty proved to be impossible, and Nixon, aware that he was living on borrowed time, requested an interim summit to be held in Switzerland in October 1974. It was not to be. Nixon was forced to bow to the inevitable and on 9th August 1974 he resigned rather than face impeachment proceedings. The only gain for disarmament was an ABM protocol that further restricted ABM deployment to the 'National Command Authorities' or, more simply, Washington and Moscow.

The disarmament torch passed to President Ford in 1974–77 and President Carter in 1977–81, but it burned less brightly as in the United States opposition increased to a Soviet Union that was steadily matching US nuclear capability. Consequently, when Ford and Brezhnev met at Vladivostok in November 1974, Ford would only enter into an interim agreement that extended SALT I by agreeing limits to MIRV technology. The number of launchers was fixed at 2400, with MIRV limited to a maximum of 1320 launchers.

However, détente all but disappeared between 1974 and 1979 and the American focus returned to defence rather than disarmament. In November 1976 the Senate Committee on the 'Present Danger' objected to SALT II and predicted a 'window of opportunity' in the late 1970s when the Soviet Union would establish not parity but an advantage over the United States. This fear was based on the fact that SALT II did not specify any restriction to the number of warheads placed on a single missile. The US Minuteman carried three warheads but the Soviet SS18 could carry up to ten and returned the United States to the 1960s fear of a 'missile gap'. However, by 1979 the US lead in MIRV technology had boosted the number of US nuclear warheads to an estimated 10,800, compared to 6571 for the Soviet Union. The Soviet Union in turn objected to the US development of new weapons systems particularly the cruise missile, B1 bomber, neutron bomb and MX missile, but to the United States they were simply qualitative rather than quantitative improvements.

The relationship between Brezhnev and President Carter deteriorated sharply in 1977 when Carter attempted to renegotiate the SALT II Treaty with a proposal for 'deep cuts' to the numbers of ICBMs deployed. The proposal was rejected by Brezhnev as ICBMs represented approximately 72 per cent of Soviet nuclear forces, compared to only 25 per cent of US nuclear forces. In June 1978 Carter bluntly warned the Soviet Union to choose between confrontation and détente.

Despite these barriers to disarmament, Carter and Brezhnev did sign the SALT II Treaty in Vienna on 18th June 1979. Both super-powers recognised the benefits of ending the arms race by observing a joint restriction to 2250 launch vehicles, with MIRV restricted to 1320 missiles. However, to counter the danger posed by improvements in strike accuracy, Carter authorised the development of the mobile MX missile, which by random position changes was planned to be less vulnerable to attack. Simultaneously, in Europe, the Soviet Union upgraded its SS4 and SS5 IRBMs with the longer-range SS20. NATO vigorously complained of an upset to the military balance in Europe and responded with plans for cruise and Pershing II missiles.

The fear of Soviet nuclear superiority and the Soviet challenge in the Third World between 1975 and 1980 raised opposition to disarmament. Finally, after the Soviet invasion of Afghanistan in December 1979, the commitment to disarmament faltered and the hawks on both sides looked to rearmament.

A crisis of confidence ended the disarmament process and a world that had grown comfortable with détente and disarmament supported widespread peace protests against the renewal of the arms race.

Questions

1. Identify and evaluate the disarmament successes of the 1970s. How successful was the disarmament process by 1979?
2. Why did disarmament come to a premature end?

ANALYSIS (2): WHY DID DISARMAMENT IN EUROPE FAIL BETWEEN 1970 AND 1980

The political breakthrough in European relations represented by French détente and German Ostpolitik raised expectations for disarmament in Europe, but ultimately Europe was to rearm rather than disarm.

The failure to agree European frontiers at Yalta and Potsdam in 1945 and the division of Europe between 1945 and 1948 raised the fear of the extension of Soviet influence throughout Europe. The Soviet threat to Berlin in June 1948 confirmed the worst fears of the Allies and the resource demands of the Berlin Airlift of 1948–49 emphasised the need for a US defence commitment to Europe. The result was the formation of NATO in April 1949 as a permanent defence force for Western Europe. The members of NATO (United States, Canada, Britain, France, Norway, Denmark, Holland, Belgium, Luxembourg, Portugal, Italy and Iceland) pledged to resist any Soviet encroachment on Western Europe in a policy of collective security. This was a significant departure for US foreign policy and led to a major US military presence in Europe and protestations from the Soviet Union. The Soviet writer Vadim Nekrasov condemned NATO as a military organisation, 'conceived primarily as an instrument for preparing war against the USSR'.[7] The foundation of West Germany in May 1949 stirred the Soviet fear of German revanchism, particularly when, according to Nekrasov, 'denazification came to a standstill'.[8] The Allies, anxious to rebuild West Germany rapidly, had quietly expunged the Nazi backgrounds of many officials and industrialists.

In May 1954 the admittance of West Germany to NATO confirmed both Soviet fears and within a week the Soviet Union announced the formation of the Warsaw Pact. This united all of the states of Eastern Europe into a single military command and combined the forces of Poland, East Germany, Czechoslovakia, Hungary, Bulgaria and Romania. Consequently, after 1954 Europe was transformed into an armed camp as NATO and the Warsaw Pact faced each other across the Iron Curtain. In this volatile situation there was no immediate prospect of disarmament or even political agreement.

The United States rejected the regular Soviet proposals for a European Security Council, wary of entering into any discussions with the Soviet Union that might legitimise the Soviet military occupation of Eastern Europe. It was only after the success of French détente, German Ostpolitik and the superpower SALT process that European disarmament became a realistic goal.

The Soviet proposal for a European Security Council was finally accepted, and in July 1973 the Helsinki Conference was convened to discuss and review European frontiers. In parallel to the political discussions in Helsinki the Mutual Balanced Force Reduction (MBFR) talks were convened in Vienna in October 1973 as a forum for European disarmament. However, whereas political agreement was reached in August 1975 with the signing of the Helsinki Accords, there was no comparative breakthrough in the disarmament talks. President Ford, in welcoming the Helsinki Accords, commented, 'the United States stands ready to demonstrate flexibility in moving these negotiations [MBFR] forward if others will do the same'.[9]

The MBFR talks had become bogged down in the complexities of defining the European theatre, the balance of forces and the technical minutiae of the comparability of weapon systems. In terms of counting soldiers, a standard Soviet division had approximately 11,000 soldiers, a British division 13,000 and a US division 16,000, but a host of variations existed according to the type of division deployed, whether mechanised or front line or support. The regular rotation of divisions, the existence of border units and the stationing of divisions immediately outside the boundaries of the European theatre all made it impossible to agree on the size of Warsaw Pact and NATO forces. Counting tanks was an easier proposition. The Warsaw Pact accepted that it had a clear three to one, advantage in tanks over NATO but argued that the NATO investment in tank-buster A-10 ground-attack aircraft and helicopters and shoulder-held anti-tank missile launchers gave a military balance. The Warsaw Pact also heavily outnumbered NATO in aircraft, but NATO possessed a qualitative advantage in aircraft speed and armament, detection and weapons-guidance radar and anti-aircraft missile batteries.

To a large extent, NATO accepted the quality over quantity argument not just in equipment but in the deployment of professional well-trained soldiers against the Warsaw Pact's poorly trained conscript divisions. However, there was apprehension in NATO circles that the Warsaw Pact would be prepared to trade high losses for conquest in a future war. The Warsaw Pact also had the advantage of common military equipment across its member nations whereas NATO members deployed different weapon systems that all required different spare parts and ammunition. Consequently, round after round of talks ended in frustration as both sides traded the advantages and disadvantages of the different conventional weapons systems.

The discussion of nuclear weapons produced even greater acrimony. To defeat a Warsaw Pact advance and especially mass tank formations, NATO reserved the right to the first use of 'battlefield' nuclear weapons. NATO possessed approximately 7000 'battlefield' warheads in the form of land mines, artillery shells, short-range missiles and bombs, compared to an estimated 3500 warheads for the Warsaw Pact. However, the Soviet Union also deployed SS4 and SS5 Intermediate Range Ballistic Missiles (IRBMs), which caused considerable NATO protest. The Soviet Union defended the missiles as defence against the French IRBM force and the SLBMs in French, British and US submarines lying off the European coast. NATO rejected this equation as the French and British nuclear forces were 'independent' nuclear deterrents outside direct NATO command. France, in particular, had withdrawn all of her military forces from NATO and forced NATO military headquarters to relocate to Belgium. However, all that mattered to the Soviet-Union was that the missiles pointed east.

These differences and disputes over the strength and composition of conventional and nuclear forces condemned the MFBR talks to endless exchanges of rhetorical formulas for disarmament. In comparison, the Strategic Arms Limitation Talks (SALT) dealt with only two clearly defined weapons systems: the ICBM and the ABM. The only successes of the period were agreements to provide advance notification of military manoeuvres and to the exchange of military observers.

After 1976 the MBFR talks were overshadowed by the slowdown in superpower détente and by the US proposal to add the neutron bomb to NATO's arsenal. The neutron bomb appeared to provide a solution to the twisted logic of the NATO defence strategy, which in order to defend Europe would destroy Europe with nuclear weapons. The enhanced radiation and reduced blast (neutron) bomb limited nuclear destruction as it sharply reduced the blast effect in favour of intense short-lived gamma radiation. NATO welcomed a bomb that in theory would kill the crews of advancing Warsaw Pact tanks yet destroy little of the surrounding area. The Soviet Union launched a propaganda offensive against the 'capitalist' bomb that would kill people but leave property intact and stirred a bitter war of words and mass protests in the West from peace campaigners, especially a revitalised Campaign for Nuclear Disarmament (CND). President Carter ended the controversy by cancelling the neutron bomb in April 1977, much to the irritation of NATO, which had actively defended the bomb against the tide of public protest.

The Soviet Union accused NATO of dragging out the MBFR talks, 'while at the same time building up its military potential in Europe'.[10] At the G7 meeting of world industrial leaders in May 1977 President Carter highlighted the growing stalemate by stating, 'the Warsaw Pact conventional forces . . . are much stronger than needed for defensive purpose'.[11]

The rise of political dissent in Eastern Europe also reduced the prospects for disarmament as the Warsaw Pact mobilised for possible military interventions. Events in Poland were returning to crisis point after a 'Great Leap Forward' in living standards promised in 1970 failed to materialise. In 1976 open protests renewed the demands for political as well as economic reform. The Roman Catholic Church identified itself with the protesters and became a focal point for dissent, and in October 1978 the appointment of a Polish Pope, John Paul II, encouraged opposition to the Soviet Union. The plight of the Polish people attracted Western support and increased the tension between NATO and the Warsaw Pact.

The hopes for European disarmament finally collapsed in 1979 as both sides entered into a new missile race. In April 1979 NATO objected to the deployment of the SS20 IRBM by the Soviet Union, citing it as an attempt to intimidate Europe. To the Soviet Union, it was a simple matter of replacing the ageing 1960s-era SS4 and SS5 IRBMs: 'the old missiles had to be replaced as their service life had expired'.[12]

NATO proposed to counter the new threat with the deployment of cruise and Pershing II missiles but provoked a storm of protest from a public reluctant to abandon the hope for disarmament. In October 1979 Brezhnev offered to reduce the number of SS20 missiles and made a unilateral cut in Warsaw Pact conventional forces of 1000 tanks and 20,000 soldiers but it was too late to save disarmament. In December 1979 NATO voted to deploy 108 Pershing II missiles and

464 cruise missiles in Europe to even the nuclear balance. The British government accepted 160 cruise missiles to be stationed at Greenham Common and Molesworth air bases and attracted intense public hostility, with the women's peace camp at Greenham Common becoming a focal point of protest. Holland and Belgium later withdrew approval for cruise missiles in the face of sustained public protest. However, within NATO the debate was no longer over disarmament but rather the level of rearmament necessary to match an estimated 600 SS20 Soviet missiles.

As the new Cold War began, people began to fear a nuclear war and a rash of books on the theme of the Third World War appeared. Europe, in particular, given advances in 'battlefield' nuclear weapons, feared a 'limited' nuclear war that would destroy European civilisation.

The failure of European disarmament was highlighted by Admiral of the Fleet Earl Mountbatten, the retired chief of the British Defence Staff, who openly condemned the move towards rearmament. In a widely quoted speech given in Strasbourg in 1979 he stated, 'the world now stands on the brink of the final abyss. Let us all resolve to take all possible steps to ensure that we do not through our own folly go over the edge.'[13]

Ultimately, disarmament in Europe failed because of the complexity of establishing an agreed military balance and through a mutual fear of invasion.

Questions

1. Why were the Warsaw Pact and NATO convinced of an invasion threat?
2. How balanced was the military balance in Europe?

SOURCES

1. SALT NEGOTIATIONS

Source A: SALT I Treaty.

On 26th May 1972 the United States and the Soviet Union signed the first Strategic Arms Limitation Talks Treaty (SALT I).

The parties undertake not to start construction of additional fixed land-based intercontinental ballistic missiles (ICBM) launchers after July 1, 1972 . . . The Parties undertake to continue active negotiations for limitations on strategic offensive arms . . . This Interim Agreement shall remain in force for a period of five years unless replaced earlier by an agreement on more complete measures limiting strategic offensive arms.

Source B: failure of SALT II.

President Nixon recorded in his memoirs the failure to sign a SALT II Treaty at the Moscow Summit of June 1974.

The wrangling went on for almost an hour. Suddenly Brezhnev looked across the table at me. In a heavy voice he said, 'Mr President, let me say that if what Dr Kissinger has outlined is his last word on this subject, there is no basis for agreement . . . He [Brezhnev] put his arm around me and said, 'We must do something of vast historical importance. We want every Russian and every American to be friends . . .' On the boat I had said to Brezhnev that our goal must be the reduction of nukes and Brezhnev responded, 'We must destroy the evil we have created.'

Source C: SALT II.

President Carter confirmed his intention to sign the SALT II Treaty in his State of the Nation address of January 1979.

Ten years ago, the United States and the Soviet Union made the historic decision to open the strategic arms limitation talks, or SALT. The purpose of SALT, then as now, is not to gain a unilateral advantage for either nation, but to protect the security of both nations, to reverse the costly and dangerous momentum of the nuclear arms race, to preserve a stable balance of nuclear forces and to demonstrate to a concerned world that we are determined to help preserve the peace . . . I will sign no agreement which does not enhance our national security . . . I will sign no agreement which cannot be verified . . . I will sign no agreement unless our deterrent force will remain overwhelming.

Source D: Soviet criticism.

Valim Zagladin, a member of the Central Committee of the CPSU, blamed the United States for the decision not to ratify the SALT II Treaty in 1980.

Immediately after the SALT II Treaty was signed the Soviet Union said that it was ready to start SALT III talks as soon as SALT II came into force . . . However, scarcely had the SALT II Treaty been signed than influential forces in the USA set about discrediting it. It was not without connivance of the US ruling circles that obstacles began to be erected in the way of the ratification of the treaty while some members of the American right-wing forces demanded that it be repudiated altogether.

Questions

1. What fear is implicit in the phrase 'unilateral advantage' in Source C?
*2. How far does Source A indicate that SALT I was the starting point for disarmament?
3. How does the language and tone of Source B convey that Brezhnev was strongly committed to disarmament?
4. In what ways do Sources C and D confirm that there was anxiety in the United States over the terms of SALT II?
5. Considering the evidence of all four sources and your own knowledge, answer the following question: Why did the commitment to disarmament in the SALT I Treaty falter and collapse by 1980?

Worked answer

*2. The text of the SALT I Treaty (Source A) clearly indicates that it is to be considered as a starting point for disarmament. The treaty is referred to as an 'Interim Agreement' and the reference is made to an undertaking to 'continue active negotiations'. There is clear evidence that future treaties are expected as SALT I will remain in force for five years, 'unless replaced earlier'. Overall the impression given is of optimism for the future, with SALT I very much the start of disarmament rather than an end in itself.

SOURCES

2. THE EUROPEAN BALANCE

Source E: NATO threat assessment.

The Final Communiqué of the NATO Foreign Ministers' Nuclear Planning Group, 24–25th April 1979, addressed the threat of the new SS20 Soviet IRBM in Europe.

Ministers took note of the extensive improvements the Soviets are making in their long-range theatre nuclear forces threatening NATO Europe, especially the

SS20 missile which affords improvements over previous systems in providing greater accuracy and more mobility and in having multiple warheads on each missile . . . Ministers reaffirmed that NATO could not rely on conventional forces alone for credible deterrence in Europe . . . it would be necessary to maintain and modernise theatre nuclear forces . . . No decisions were taken at this stage.

Source F: Soviet defence of SS20 missiles.

The Soviet press agency Novosti published the following defence of the decision to deploy SS20 missiles in Europe.

The development and deployment of the SS20 missiles can be explained by a number of quite specific military, technical and political factors. From a purely technical standpoint, the old missiles had to be replaced as their service life had expired. They were already twenty years old. Not to replace would have meant that the Soviet Union would be left without that type of weapon . . . NATO has US forward-based nuclear weapons (F-111 and F-4 aircraft and carrier-based A-6 and A-7 aircraft) and also British and French nuclear systems. Britain has 64 Polaris missiles and France has 98 missiles and 44 Mirage-4 bombers.

Source G: NATO deployment of cruise missiles.

On 12th December 1979 a special meeting of the foreign and defence ministers of NATO approved a decision to upgrade NATO's nuclear deterrent.

The Warsaw Pact has over the years developed a large and growing capability in nuclear systems that directly threaten Western Europe . . . These trends have prompted serious concern within the alliance because if they were to continue Soviet superiority in theatre nuclear systems would undermine the stability achieved in inter-continental systems . . . Accordingly the Ministers have decided to modernise NATO's Long Range Theatre Nuclear Forces by the deployment in Europe of US ground-launched systems comprising 108 Pershing II launchers which would replace existing Pershing I-A and 464 Ground Launched Cruise Missiles all with single warheads.

Source H: Mountbatten's Strasbourg speech.

Earl Mountbatten, Admiral of the Fleet, condemned the renewed arms race in a speech in Strasbourg in 1979.

I am deeply saddened when I reflect on how little has been achieved in spite of all the talk there has been, particularly about nuclear disarmament. There have been numerous international conferences and negotiations on the subject and we have all nursed dreams of a world at peace but to no avail . . . As a military man who has given half a century of active service I say in all sincerity that the nuclear arms race has no military purpose. Wars cannot be fought with nuclear weapons . . . The world now stands on the brink of the final abyss. Let us all resolve to take all practical steps to ensure that we do not, through our own folly, go over the edge.

Questions

1. What underlying fear is expressed by the phrase 'credible deterrence' in Source E?
*2. According to the evidence of Sources E and G, why did NATO object to the SS20 missile?
3. Compare and contrast the positions of NATO and the Soviet Union as given in Sources E, F and G. What facts do each ignore to their advantage?
4. In what ways do Sources E and H differ on the value of nuclear weapons?
5. Considering all four Sources E to H and your own knowledge, answer the following question: How far was NATO correct that the SS20 altered the balance of European military forces?

Worked answer

*2. Source E provides three precise objections to the Soviet deployment of SS20 missiles: namely, 'greater accuracy', 'more mobility' and the fact the SS20 carries 'multiple warheads'. Source G concentrates upon the broader danger of the SS20, granting 'Soviet superiority' in the European theatre and the related danger of 'undermining' the SALT agreements. The importance of the nuclear deterrent to NATO is stressed in Source E as NATO cannot 'rely upon conventional forces alone'. This point highlights the superiority of Warsaw Pact forces and NATO's reliance on the nuclear deterrent for the defence of Europe. Source G supports this concern by noting that the SS20 is part of 'a large and growing capability' in theatre nuclear weapons. Consequently, NATO's overall objection to the SS20 is that it will confer superiority in nuclear weapons which when added to the Soviet superiority in conventional forces will seriously alter the balance of power in Europe.

7

EVIL EMPIRE

BACKGROUND NARRATIVE

Ronald Reagan was elected president of the United States in November 1980, after an election campaign that rejected détente and disarmament. Reagan was convinced that Presidents Ford and Carter had been negligent in the security of the United States and that the Soviet Union had achieved not parity of nuclear arms but superiority. He was lambasted for his simplicity of approach to foreign affairs but many warmed to his simple homespun philosophy of American good versus Soviet evil.

Reagan authorised a massive expansion of US nuclear and conventional forces while at the same time challenging the Soviet Union to end the arms race in Intermediate Nuclear Forces (INF) talks and Strategic Arms Reduction Talks (START).

On 11th November 1982 Leonid Brezhnev died and was replaced as the general secretary of the Communist Party of the Soviet Union (CPSU) by Yuri Andropov. Andropov attempted to counter the US arms build-up with a peace offensive but the Soviet Union was in economic crisis and Andropov's priority was domestic reform.

The renewal of the Cold War caused widespread public fear. Films like *Threads* in 1982 graphically portrayed the effects of a nuclear war and encouraged a mass membership of peace organisations.

On 8th March 1983 President Reagan, in a speech in Orlando, Florida, described the Soviet union as an 'evil empire', and on 23rd March 1983 he announced the Strategic Defense Initiative (SDI) to research anti-ballistic missile defences. The sense of imminent war increased on 31st August 1983 when Korean Airlines passenger flight KAL 007 strayed into Soviet airspace and was shot down without warning.

President Reagan eased the tension in January 1984 with a conciliatory speech, but before there could be any dialogue with the Soviet Union Yuri Andropov died from kidney failure on 9th February 1984. The new Soviet leader, Konstantin Chernenko, was seventy-three and in poor health. He died on 10th March 1985 from emphysema.

The next day Mikhail Gorbachev was appointed general secretary of the CPSU and paved the way for the end of the Cold War with the policy of glasnost.

ANALYSIS (1): WHY AND HOW DID PRESIDENT REAGAN CHALLENGE THE SOVIET UNION FROM 1981 TO 1985?

President Reagan was a conviction politician who was determined to revitalise the United States after years of perceived weakness and to confront the expansion of communism from a Soviet Union he characterised as the 'evil empire'. Reagan unleashed a verbal and military challenge against the Soviet Union between 1981 and 1985. To detractors, his hostile stance made war more likely, whereas to his supporters, Reagan was a plain-speaking hero whose policies hastened the end of the Cold War.

Reagan had no experience of foreign affairs and in the opinion of Zimmerman he became President in November 1980 armed with, 'a vision and a few simple maxims'.[1] Reagan's vision was to 'bring about a spiritual revival in America'[2] aimed at the restoration of national pride and confidence at a time when the United States appeared to be failing. The US economy was in depression, with interest rates, inflation and unemployment all at record highs. The defeat in Vietnam had scarred and divided American society and tarnished the reputation of the US forces. The sense of military impotency was further increased in April 1980 by the failure of a military rescue mission to free the fifty-two Americans held hostage in the US embassy in Iran. In addition, the rapid expansion of the Soviet Union's nuclear capability between 1975 and 1980 led to a belief that the United States was vulnerable to a Soviet nuclear attack. There was also a pronounced fear of an eventual world communist victory as communism spread into Afghanistan, Angola, Ethiopia, Cambodia, and (of most concern) Nicaragua and El

Salvador on the US doorstep. In particular, US defence analysts interpreted Afghanistan as a Soviet stepping stone to the Persian Gulf in a bid to control the oil fields of the Middle East.

The overall assessment was of 'America in retreat' and it propelled President Reagan into the offensive. On 29th January 1981, during his first presidential press conference, President Reagan defined communist philosophy as the 'right to commit any crime, to lie, to cheat'.[3] His words ended détente and returned the Cold War to the language of Truman and the confrontation of the 1950s. Reagan subsequently dismissed détente as a Soviet licence to 'pursue whatever policies of subversion, aggression and expansionism they wanted anywhere in the world'.[4] In Great Britain Prime Minister Margaret Thatcher held similar views and Reagan and Thatcher formed a formidable anti-Soviet coalition.

Reagan had no concrete foreign policy aims and it was left to Secretary of State Alexander Haig to specify the 'four pillars' of US foreign policy. The fourth pillar addressed the need for 'greater Soviet restraint and greater Soviet reciprocity'.[5] The only reciprocity that subsequently emerged was the exchange of icy letters between Brezhnev and Reagan.

The immediate issue for President Reagan was to counter the rise of the communist Sandinista government in Nicaragua in 1981, and a communist challenge to the government of El Salvador. Reagan firmly believed that the Soviet Union and Cuba were behind a plot to spread communism throughout South America. Congress and the wider American public rejected this analysis and in his autobiography Reagan admitted his failure to 'convince the American people of the seriousness of the threat we faced from Marxist guerrillas in central America'.[6] Congress feared another Vietnam and refused to vote funds for a US military intervention. Reagan was undeterred and used the CIA to channel covert military and financial support to the anti-communist Contra 'freedom fighters'. The result was the censure of the Reagan administration by Congress in 1984 and by the International Court of Human Rights in 1986 for funding a war in which an estimated 60,000 civilians were murdered by right-wing death squads. There was also considerable controversy when it was revealed that illegal funds had been raised by Colonel Oliver North through the sale of arms to Iran. The Iran–Contra scandal rocked the presidency in 1986. However, in the absence of direct evidence of presidential authorisation Reagan survived the scandal.

The most potent challenge to the Soviet Union was the approval of a vast 53 per cent increase in US defence spending in October 1981, which represented the biggest military build-up in US peacetime history. The B1 bomber and the neutron bomb programmes cancelled by President Carter were restored and approval was given for the development of Stealth aircraft, which were designed to be invisible to enemy radar. The US Navy was one of the biggest beneficiaries with approval for an increase in carrier groups from twelve to fifteen. The aim was for the establishment of a 600-ship navy to guarantee the 'horizontal' projection of US firepower world-wide. The only problematic part of the military expansion was the deployment of the mobile MX missile as a replacement to the fixed-silo Minuteman missile. Technical and environmental arguments dogged the MX programme. Eventually, after over thirty 'basing' proposals were considered, the MX was quietly deployed into the 'vulnerable' Minuteman silos it was designed to replace.

The military build-up was condemned by the Soviet Union and peace campaigners, including Reagan's own daughter, Patti. The Soviet Union pressed for a renewal of arms control talks, and on 18th November 1981 President Reagan proposed Intermediate Nuclear Forces (INF) talks and the Strategic Arms Reduction Talks (START). Reagan captured world headlines with the Zero Option for Europe. This was a proposal for the removal of Soviet SS20 missiles from Europe in return for no future deployment of US cruise and Pershing II missiles. The Soviet Union rejected the proposal as a one-sided zero as it ignored French and British nuclear missiles and US 'forward-based' F111 strategic aircraft. There was also no START progress as the Soviet Union refused to contemplate 50 per cent 'deep cuts' to ICBM forces in isolation from the US advantage in SLBM and strategic bomber forces.

To critics, the US proposals were designed for public consumption to deflect criticism away from the arms build-up and were calculated for Soviet rejection. To supporters, the military challenge was essential to restore the military balance and was a deliberate Reagan strategy to stretch and break the fragile Soviet economy.

The Reagan administration was divided between 'squeezers' and 'dealers'. The squeezers, led by Secretary of Defense Caspar Weinberger and the director of the CIA, Bill Casey, wanted to squeeze the Soviet economy into overspend. The dealers, were represented by George Shultz, who replaced Haig as secretary of state in June 1982, and they favoured negotiation. The commitment to the Strategic Defense Initiative (SDI) in 1983 was a policy of squeeze, but the later entry into summit negotiations was a dealer's agenda. Gorbachev was later to complain that Reagan's freedom to negotiate was hampered by the US Defense Department, which opposed the 'slightest hint at a thaw in relations'.[7]

Reagan renewed his verbal assault on the Soviet Union in March 1982 with a prediction that Marxism would be left on the 'ashheap of history'.[8] He repeated this prediction in a speech to the British Houses of Parliament on 8th June 1982, and in a comprehensive critique of the Soviet Union warned against any accommodation with 'totalitarian evil'.[9]

The response from the Soviet Union was muted by the sharp decline in Brezhnev's health, and he died on 11th November 1982 after a period of rule notorious for the stagnation of the Soviet economy. The reality of daily life in the Soviet Union was bare subsistence, and in Eastern Europe (and Poland, in particular) there was widespread political dissent. The Politburo appointed Yuri Andropov as the new general secretary of the CPSU and his more liberal regime revealed mounting evidence of economic weakness. Nevertheless, the United States remained convinced of a Soviet threat. Shultz recommended a softer line and questioned the CIA reports that 'painted a picture of a mighty nation confronting us everywhere . . . the picture they conjured up of the Soviet Union did not match the reality I saw'.[10]

Andropov attempted to blunt US hostility with a peace offensive designed to capitalise on the widespread peace protests in the Western world, which included the moral condemnation of the arms race by the Catholic bishops of the United States. In June 1982 over 700,000 people crammed into Central Park, New York, to demand a nuclear freeze. Soviet propaganda supported the peace movement and expressed the fear that the United States was preparing 'blueprints for total confrontation with the Soviet Union'.[11] The protests were heightened in June 1982 when President Reagan rejected the compromise 'walk in the woods' deal between the US and Soviet INF negotiators Nitze and Kvitsinsky. The Pentagon also publicly released a defence paper that contained a strategy for winning a protracted nuclear war and Reagan openly referred to the prospect of fighting a limited nuclear war in Europe.

President Reagan's challenge to the Soviet Union reached its zenith on 8th March 1983 when he described the Soviet Union as an 'evil empire' and the 'focus of all evil in the modern world'.[12] This was followed on 23rd March by the announcement of the Strategic Defense Initiative (SDI) on national television by President Reagan. World opinion was excited by the vision of a laser defence shield in space that would make nuclear missiles 'impotent and obsolete'.[13] It was a media gift and endless visual graphics soon resulted in the appellation 'Star

Wars'. However, there was no scientific breakthrough and SDI was more science fiction than science fact. The research prospects were so poor that on the same day as Reagan made his announcement Major-General Lamberson testified to a Senate committee: 'we would not recommend an acceleration at this point'.[14] Reagan was attracted to SDI by its political potential. As a defensive programme it immediately wrongfooted the protests of the Soviet Union, the peace campaign and the Catholic bishops. The announcement was also timed to match the passage of Reagan's military budget through Congress, and according to Zimmerman its primary purpose was 'to help defense budgets over [their] congressional hurdles'.[15]

The Soviet Union condemned SDI as a breach of the 1972 Anti-Ballistic Missile Treaty and a US attempt to neutralise the Soviet Strategic Rocket Force. However, the issue was lost in a torrent of anti-Soviet anger on 31st August 1983 when Soviet Air Command destroyed Korean Airlines flight KAL 007 after it strayed off course into Soviet airspace. All 269 passengers and crew were killed and the incident justified to many people Reagan's charge of an 'evil empire'. It also indicated the tense state of the Soviet armed forces.

The moral victory over communism was reinforced in October 1983 with a military victory when US marines stormed ashore in Grenada, ostensibly to protect American medical students caught up in a coup, but in practice to prevent the formation of a new Marxist government. The swift victory enhanced Reagan's reputation as a robust leader who had forced communism into retreat. It also earned bitter criticism from Prime Minister Thatcher who had not been consulted in advance about the decision to invade a member nation of the British Commonwealth.

The challenge to the Soviet Union intensified in November 1983 with the confirmation of the imminent deployment of cruise and Pershing II missiles in Europe. In protest, the USSR withdrew from the INF talks and START. Andropov's peace offensive had failed, but in January 1984 Reagan offered an olive branch of further talks. It was an election year and Reagan was conscious of the need to soften his image, but he was also convinced that his challenge to the Soviet Union had successfully thwarted Soviet ambitions. The offer came too late for Andropov, who died from kidney failure on 9th February 1984, to be replaced as general secretary by Konstantin Chernenko. Reagan was re-elected in November 1984 and a summit with Chernenko was scheduled for 12th March 1985. However, two days before the scheduled date, Chernenko died from emphysema and the Politburo elected the reformist Mikhail Gorbachev as general secretary of the CPSU. The confrontation faded as Reagan felt increasingly confident of the military superiority of the United States. He began to speak of peace and security and warmed to the open, friendly statements of Gorbachev.

Reagan's challenge to communism was an ideological crusade against a system that he firmly believed threatened world freedom, but whereas his actions certainly 'made Americans walk tall again', his blunt confrontation risked nuclear war.

Questions

1. How justified was President Reagan's accusation that the Soviet Union was an 'evil empire'?
2. To what extent did the 'squeezers' influence President Reagan's foreign policy?

ANALYSIS (2): HOW CAPABLE WAS THE SOVIET UNION OF SUSTAINING THE COLD WAR?

Soviet propaganda as late as 1989 propagated the image of an advanced Soviet superpower on the threshold of eclipsing capitalism. However, the reality was of a nation in economic decline, racked by internal dissent and in no position to sustain the Cold War.

Leonid Brezhnev died in November 1982 after presiding over the Soviet Union for eighteen years. He was a remote leader who enjoyed the fruits of position that gave rise to the following apocryphal story. Brezhnev's mother visited his luxury home. She was highly impressed with it, the swimming pool and the fleet of cars, and over dinner she was shown pictures of his country dacha, a holiday home on the Black Sea, a private plane and a yacht. 'Well, what do you think?' asked Brezhnev. 'I'm worried in case the Bolsheviks return,' replied his mother.

Brezhnev's rule had 'created the conditions for the growth of a truly privileged elite'[16] and the result was the division of Soviet society into two classes – the 19 million members of the Communist Party and the remainder of the population. The Communist Party of the Soviet Union (CPSU), and in particular its vast army of bureaucrats, the nomenklatura, governed every aspect of life in the Soviet Union. At national, regional and local levels the nomenklatura also enjoyed the fruits of office according to their individual status and position, which included access to private shops, private hospitals, limousines, country dachas and exclusive holiday resorts. During his final years, Brezhnev had attempted to address the problems of the abuses of power by the nomenklatura. The chairman of the KGB, Yuri Andropov, was placed in charge of an anti-corruption campaign in 1980 but, to the embarrassment of Brezhnev, the KGB arrested his daughter Galina and son-in-law, the deputy minister of the interior, on charges of diamond smuggling and currency speculation. They were demoted but many others were executed for diverting budgets, for private gain, in a series of scams that discredited the CPSU.

Consequently, Andropov was the natural choice to replace Brezhnev as the general secretary of the CPSU in the expectation that he would have the necessary authority to restore the credibility of the Party. His credentials were enhanced by the fact that he lived in a two-roomed flat and eschewed the trappings of office. Andropov planned to reform the CPSU and to tackle three major problems that were sapping the ability of the Soviet Union to sustain the Cold War: namely, economic decline, separatism and human rights. These problems transcended the Cold War and ultimately threatened the survival of the USSR as they called into question the legitimacy and benefits of the communist system. Andropov acknowledged this reality in an article in *Kommunist* in March 1983 when he admitted that 'Soviet society did not match Marx's idea of the socialist future'.[17]

The renewed Cold War was an unwelcome distraction from these pressing problems and one that Andropov attempted to resolve through the declaration of a peace offensive on 21st December 1982. Andropov condemned the 'war preparations of the United States and the NATO bloc'[18] and offered an immediate 25 per cent reduction in strategic weapons coupled with a freeze on nuclear-weapons development. The offer was rejected but Andropov hoped that public pressure from the burgeoning peace movement in the West would force the United States and NATO to scale down the arms race and block the deployment of cruise and Pershing II missiles to Europe. However, the elections across Europe in 1982 disappointed Andropov. In Britain the electorate rejected the nuclear-disarmament policies of the Labour Party and re-elected Margaret Thatcher as prime minister. In West Germany and France the elections also returned governments, led by Helmut Kohl and François Mitterrand, that supported the tough stance of the United States. Eventually, Andropov, in frustration at the decision to deploy cruise and Pershing II missiles in Europe, ended Soviet participation in the INF talks and START in November 1983. It was a superpower stalemate.

Throughout the 1980s the Soviet press agency Novosti flooded the West with a series of booklets that were designed to maintain the image of a powerful superpower. The reality was of a USSR in sharp economic decline. The 1967 guide to the Soviet Union proclaimed the USSR as one of the 'world's most advanced states' and predicted 'a 47–50 per cent increase in the volume of industrial output'.[19] This was the rise of the communist planned economy that Khrushchev had boasted in 1959 would 'bury' the United States. Instead, the annual growth rates for industrial output dropped steadily from an estimated 5.25 per cent in 1967 to 2 per cent by 1980. The planned economy was failing and with it the standard of living. The reality of life in the Soviet Union in the 1970s was of empty shops, poor housing, subsistence diets, intense pollution and the return to a barter economy. The nation that boasted a space station manufactured the Lada, while in East Germany the ubiquitous Trabant was so primitive that to check the petrol level it was first necessary to park and then use a dipstick. In both cases the waiting list for delivery was seven to ten years long.

The stagnation of the Soviet economy was a product of the unrealistic targets of the Five Year Plans, poor infrastructure, the corruption of the nomenklatura, the high cost of the arms race and the over-reliance on heavy industry. In addition the workforce was guaranteed employment by the Soviet constitution and received a standard wage regardless of the quantity or quality of production. There was no incentive for workers to improve production and especially not when the average worker earned 195 roubles per month, compared to 750 roubles per month for the average member of the nomenklatura. The long working hours, poor housing, empty shops and lack of social diversions produced a population that took refuge in the vodka bottle. Much of Soviet industry was on a virtual three-day week as workers started the weekend on Friday and didn't recover until Tuesday.

Andropov made worker discipline his first target in the Parasite Law of January 1983, and while touring a factory urged the workers to avoid 'the loss of working time through absenteeism, slow work and breaks for cigarettes'.[20] Andropov simultaneously began to shake up the complacent nomenklatura. He replaced 19 out of 84 ministers, 20 per cent of the regional party chiefs, and within the Politburo promoted Mikhail Gorbachev.

The separatist issue was perhaps the greatest challenge facing Andropov and later Gorbachev as it threatened the structure of the USSR. The first line of the Soviet national anthem proclaimed 'the unbreakable union of freeborn republics'[21] Soviet propaganda as late as 1986 boasted of '100 peoples as one family'[22] and glorified ethnic diversity and respect for different cultures. In practice, most republics had been 'Russified' with the appointment of Russian officials to important administrative posts and primacy accorded to the Russian language and culture. The Soviet constitution permitted 'the right freely to secede from the USSR'[23] but in reality the Brezhnev Doctrine dictated the limits of independence. The Soviet Army, rather than fraternal brotherhood, bound the republics together. By 1980, the Soviet Union was in separatist crisis. Poland, with the rise of Solidarity, was in open revolt. Romania, Hungary and Bulgaria were distancing themselves from Russian leadership. The Baltic States, Ukraine and Georgia were demanding independence and protesters routinely burned the Soviet flag. The rise of Islam and the Russian invasion of Afghanistan also intensified opposition to Soviet rule in the predominately Muslim republics of the southern USSR. Separatism threatened the USSR with dissolution, but, paradoxically, the renewed Cold War promoted unity against the external enemy.

The campaign for human rights, particularly free speech, was also a significant threat to the stability of the Soviet Union. The Helsinki Accords of 1975 had guaranteed freedom of speech and protest but the CPSU soon found it to be an uncomfortable experience. The simple accusation of dissidents that communism wasn't working found a deep resonance among ordinary people trapped in endless queues to secure the basic necessities of life, or alternatively paying bribes to jump the queue. The Soviet constitution defined human rights in terms of the benefits of the communist system and as late as 1986 Soviet propaganda boasted, 'in the USSR there are no unemployed, homeless, illiterate or people who are otherwise socially deprived'.[24] It was true that the prices of basic foodstuffs, transport and housing had been frozen since 1962 but the provision of a bare existence did not match the heady boasts of the CPSU: 'Socialism has made Russia, once a backward country, one of the world's most advanced states.'[25] The CPSU was prepared to tolerate discussion of how to improve communism but not the rejection of communism. To silence dissent, Andropov, as head of the KGB and later general secretary, declared dissidents mentally ill and confined them to mental hospitals. The Soviet Union was subsequently suspended as a member of the World Psychiatric Association from 1984 to 1989.

The policy was indicative of the need to buy time for reform but Andropov's time had run out. In October 1983 he was rushed to hospital, had a kidney removed and thereafter never left his hospital bed. The Soviet public were informed he was suffering from a 'bad cold' but on 9th February 1984 he died from kidney failure. Days before his death Andropov endorsed Mikhail Gorbachev as the new general secretary. The endorsement was ignored by the Politburo in favour of the old Brezhnev comrade, Konstantin Chernenko. According to Richard Sakwa, 'they put their own interests above that of the country'.[26] The strategy was to batten down the hatches and to preserve the traditional authority of the CPSU. Brezhnev's daughter Galina was rehabilitated and Chernenko's supporters called for 'moderation in the speed of change'.[27] Chernenko died on 10th March 1985, and while the seventy-year-old Vicktor Grishin had his supporters among the Politburo's old guard, Gorbachev had generated sufficient support for himself. At 6.09 p.m. on 11th March 1985 he was publicly declared general secretary of the CPSU. The suspicions of the old guard proved correct, as in a speech on 17th May 1985 Gorbachev declared, 'we must all change . . . but anyone who is not prepared to do so must simply get out of our way and must not be allowed to interfere'.[28] A similar direct attitude cut the Gordian knot of the Cold War as Gorbachev dispensed with the normal Soviet rhetoric, openly admitted the mistakes of Soviet foreign policy and sought an immediate end to the Cold War with the words, 'we have embarked upon a path dedicated to bettering relations with the United States and we expect reciprocity'.[29] The United States did not realise it, but the Cold War was effectively over and the battle was on for the survival of the Soviet Union.

Soviet propaganda had skilfully concealed the scale of the decline of the country, but ultimately President Reagan, the ex-Hollywood actor, had challenged a superpower more Hollywood set than material fact.

Questions

1. Why had the Soviet economy failed to improve standards of living?
2. To what extent had the Soviet Union no choice but to end the Cold War?

SOURCES

1. THE RENEWAL OF THE COLD WAR

Source A: Reagan's challenge.

In his autobiography, published in 1990, President Reagan explained his decision to challenge the Soviet Union.

During the late seventies, I felt our country had begun to abdicate its historical role as the spiritual leader of the Free World and its foremost defender of democracy. Some of our resolve was gone, along with a part of our commitment to uphold the values we cherished. Predictably, the Soviets had interpreted our hesitation and reluctance to act . . . and had tried to exploit it to the fullest, moving ahead with their agenda to achieve a Communist-dominated world . . . The Soviets were more dedicated than ever to achieving Lenin's goal of a communist world . . . I deliberately set out to say some frank things about the Russians, to let them know there were some new fellows in Washington.

Source B: the evil empire.

On 8th March 1983 in a speech at the annual conference of the National Association of Evangelicals in Orlando, Florida, President Reagan branded the Soviet Union as an 'evil empire'.

Yes, let us pray for the salvation of all of those who live in that totalitarian darkness – pray they will discover the joy of knowing God. But until they do, let us be aware . . . they are the focus of evil in the modern world. So I urge you to speak out against those who would place the United States in a position of military and moral inferiority. I urge you to beware the temptation . . . to ignore the facts of history and the aggressive impulses of an evil empire, to simply call the arms race a giant misunderstanding and thereby remove yourself from a struggle between right and wrong and good and evil.

Source C: Andropov and the military balance.

On 27th March 1983 the general secretary of the CPSU, Yuri Andropov, issued a statement on the military balance.

It is true that the Soviet Union has strengthened its defence capability. Faced with the feverish US effort to establish military bases near Soviet territory, to develop ever new types of nuclear and other weapons, the USSR was compelled to do so in order to put an end to US military superiority for which Washington now longs so much . . . As to the allegations that the United States has done nothing in the past two decades, only naive people will believe that . . . the United States installed multiple warheads on its ballistic missiles . . . the number of nuclear warheads grew from four to over ten thousand. Can an increase in the nuclear arsenal by a factor of 2.5 be referred to as inactivity? No, it certainly cannot.

Source D: Chernenko's letter to President Reagan.

Extract from a letter from Konstantin Chernenko, general secretary of the CPSU, to President Reagan, March 1984.

I ask you, Mr President, to look at the realities of the international situation from our perspective and you will see right from the start that the Soviet Union is encircled by a chain of American military bases. What conclusions should we draw from this as to the intentions of the United States? . . . I remind you that it was the Soviet Union that offered to reduce their number to the minimum on the side of the USSR and NATO. And in response, Pershing and cruise missiles appeared in the vicinity of our borders. What would be your attitude, Mr President, had something like this happened with respect to the United States? . . . Even under these circumstances we have displayed utmost restraint.

Questions

1. Explain the phrase 'spiritual leader of the Free World' as it appears in Source A.
2. In what ways do Sources A and B support the view that President Reagan saw the Cold War as a moral crusade?
3. How far do Andropov (Source C) and Chernenko (Source D) agree on the causes of the arms race?
4. Using your own knowledge and all four sources, explain why the relationship between the Soviet Union and the United states deteriorated so rapidly between 1980 and 1985.

2. THE ECONOMIC DECLINE OF THE SOVIET UNION

Source E: Soviet economic growth.

Extract from the Soviet Novosti Press Agency booklet 'The Soviet Course', 1986.

Living standards have risen considerably in the Soviet Union over the last 25 years . . . people began to eat and dress better and the sale of durable goods to the population grew many times over . . . the USSR is among the world's leaders in the output of oil, coal, steel, machine tools and much more . . . the diversion of funds and efforts for defensive purposes because of the arms race that has been forced upon us has also played and continues to play its role . . . The economic capacity of the Soviet Union is to increase by 100% by the year 2000 . . . the task is to produce goods of better quality, faster and cheaper.

Source F: role of the Communist Party.

Extract from a resolution of the Twenty-seventh Congress of the CPSU held from 25th February to 6th March 1986.

The Communist Party of the Soviet Union is the tried and tested militant vanguard of the Soviet people which unites on a voluntary basis the more advanced politically, more conscious section of the working class, collective-farm peasantry and intelligentsia of the USSR . . . the rules stress that the Party exists for the people and serves the people and is thus the leading and guiding force in Soviet society . . . the Party attaches the greatest importance to its honour and to the struggle for purity within its ranks.

Source G: opposition to the Communist Party.

Extract from a *Guardian* newspaper report (12th September 1987) of a statement from an opposition group to the Communist Party.

Its [CPSU] ranks include people who carry responsibility for the abuses and miscalculations of the past, and who made up the rows of bureaucrats and that oppressive mass of officials, who cut themselves off from the hopes and needs of their people . . . the conference ended with calls for a momument to be built to Stalin's victims and free access for independent citizens to compete against Communist Party members in local elections.

Source H: the Soviet reality.

Extract from an *Economist* magazine report (21st November 1987) of life in the Soviet Union.

The Russians have now begun admitting some of the things they had spent those years [1970's] trying to hide. It is now clear that poor food, increasing industrial pollution, rising alcoholism and declining hygiene and medical standards have produced some alarming consequences. The statistics on infant mortality, the spread of infectious diseases and declining life expectancy make the Soviet Union look less like a superpower than a struggling Third World country . . . the Soviet Union comes a sorry 50th in the world league table of infant mortality.

Questions

1. Explain the term 'militant vanguard' as used in Source E.
2. Comment on the ways Sources E and F present a positive image of the Soviet Union.

*3. How do Sources F and G differ in their attitude to the Communist Party?

4. Using the evidence of Sources E to H and your own knowledge, explain why the Russian people lost confidence in the Communist Party of the Soviet Union.

Worked answer

*3. Sources F and G present sharply divergent attitudes to the Communist Party. Source F is the official voice of the Communist Party and the attitude promoted is of a successful leadership that 'exists for the people and serves the people'. Source G is the reported opinion of an opposition party and the attitude is challenging and strongly critical of 'abuses and miscalculations' by the Communist Party. The attitudes are entirely opposite. The Communist Party in Source F is obviously proud of its record as the 'tried and tested militant vanguard', whereas the record recalled by Source G is of 'Stalin's victims'. The portrayal of the officials of the Communist Party is also significantly different. Source F dwells upon the 'honour' and 'purity' of officials, whereas Source G refers to the 'oppressive mass of officials'. Overall, the attitudes may be summarised as promotion and praise (Source F) and condemnation and opposition (Source G).

8

GLASNOST

BACKGROUND NARRATIVE

Mikhail Gorbachev was elected general secretary of the Communist Party of the Soviet Union (CPSU) on 11th March 1985 and within weeks introduced the world to two new Russian words, glasnost and perestroika. Glasnost or 'openness' allowed for an open and honest appraisal of the problems facing the Soviet Union, including the Cold War confrontation. Perestroika or 'restructuring' addressed the need for the fundamental reform of the Soviet economy and the organisation of the CPSU.

Glasnost ended the Cold War. Gorbachev admitted the past mistakes of Soviet foreign policy, announced a Soviet withdrawal from Eastern Europe and offered major concessions to end the arms race.

President Reagan and the West were at first hesitant and wary of a new Soviet propaganda offensive, but over the course of four summits between 1985 and 1988 Reagan and Gorbachev ended the Cold War. However, disagreements over the Strategic Defense Initiative (SDI) delayed the end of the arms race to 1991.

Perestroika was less successful, and by 1988 the reforms of the economy and the Communist Party had failed to win the confidence of the Soviet people. Arguments divided the CPSU and ultimately undermined the credibility of the Party and the USSR.

In January 1989 George Bush became president of the United States. Along with the rest of the West he watched in astonishment as the Soviet Union, against all expectations, imploded between 1989 and 1991. During 1989 the states of Eastern Europe disaffiliated themselves from Soviet influence and set in motion the procedures to elect democratic governments. On 9th November 1989 the Berlin Wall was demolished as the German people, impatient for reunification, moved faster than the politicians. Within the Soviet Union the reformers and the Communist hard-liners battled for political control between 1990 and 1991. Gorbachev's authority was eroded and in August 1991 the hard-liners launched a coup to restore the authority of the CPSU. Instead, their illegal actions handed a political coup to Boris Yeltsin, the president of the Republic of Russia, who promptly banned the CPSU. The USSR collapsed in December 1991 when the individual Soviet republics opted for independence and the establishment of a new Commonwealth of Independent State (CIS).

On 25th December 1991 a triumphant Boris Yeltsin escorted Mikhail Gorbachev out of the Kremlin. The USSR and the Communist Party of the Soviet Union had come to an ignominious end and, to paraphrase T.S. Eliot, the Cold War ended not with a bang but a whimper.

ANALYSIS (1): IN WHAT WAYS DID GLASNOST END THE COLD WAR AND PRECIPITATE THE COLLAPSE OF THE USSR?

The Cold War was an ideological and military confrontation between two opposing political systems. Glasnost ended the Cold War by allowing the rejection of the Soviet imperative to compete with the West. However, by exposing the reality of life in the Soviet Union, it also triggered the collapse of the USSR.

Gorbachev's inheritance as general secretary of the Communist Party (CPSU) was a Soviet Union in sharp decline and 'ripe for change'.[1] General Secretary Andropov had exhorted the people and the CPSU to greater efforts but Gorbachev's instinct was for root and branch reform of the entire Soviet system, including relations with the West.

Gorbachev declared the rise of 'new political thinking . . . particularly in the field of disarmament'.[2] The immediate sign of 'new thinking' was the replacement of Foreign Minister Andrei Gromyko by Eduard Shevardnadze in July 1985. Gromyko had held the position for twenty-eight years and was known as 'Grim Grom' by President Reagan and 'Mr Nyet' by the United Nations for his dour defence of the Soviet Union.

Gorbachev was determined to end the drain imposed on the Soviet economy by the arms race but he also rejected Lenin's tenet of conflict with capitalism and stated, 'adversaries must become partners'.[3] At first President Reagan was suspicious and it was not until 1987 that he accepted that Gorbachev was radically altering the Soviet Union and could be trusted. In 1987 Gorbachev published *Perestroika: New Thinking for Our Country and the World* and Reagan commented that it was 'as damning as anything written about Communism in the West'.[4]

Reagan and Gorbachev met for their first summit in Geneva in November 1985 and in a media-friendly 'fireside chat' explored the prospects for disarmament. There was remarkable unanimity in the joint desire for a nuclear-free world but sharp disagreement over the Strategic Defense Initiative (SDI). Reagan regarded SDI as essential to the future security of the United States whereas Gorbachev dismissed it as a deliberate escalation of the arms race, 'the aim being to exhaust us'.[5] The Intermediate Nuclear Forces (INF) talks and the Strategic Arms Reduction Talks (START) remained deadlocked as both sides continued to be wary of each other's intentions.

Gorbachev objected in March 1986 when President Reagan, under pressure from Secretary of Defense Caspar Weinberger, breached the SALT II limitations by arming B52 bombers with air-launched cruise missiles. The US air strikes on Libya in April 1986 and the mutual expulsion of spies that September also harmed relations. Weinberger consistently opposed disarmament and lobbied for an intensification of the arms race, whereas Secretary of State George Shultz recommended negotiation. Shultz complained of an administration locked into confrontation and believed that Reagan was 'a prisoner of his own staff'.[6] Gorbachev lambasted Reagan's advisers for their 'caveman mentality'[7] and appealed to Reagan for a further summit.

The second summit was held in Reykjavik, Iceland, in October 1986 and Reagan described it as 'one of the angriest days of my life'.[8] To Reagan's fury, Gorbachev offered comprehensive disarmament concessions but conditional upon the abandonment of SDI. The summit ended in acrimony but in October 1987 Gorbachev broke the impasse in the INF talks by dropping the linkage to SDI.

At a third summit in Washington on 8th December 1987 Gorbachev and Reagan signed the Intermediate Nuclear Forces (INF) treaty or, more popularly, the Zero Option. For the first time in the Cold War an entire class of weapons was abolished as Soviet SS20s and US cruise and Pershing missiles were removed from Europe. Gorbachev made the concessions Andropov had refused to contemplate in 1983 and voluntarily extended the treaty to include Soviet Asia.

The START talks remained blocked by continued disagreements on SDI. President Reagan offered to share SDI technology fully in an 'open labs' policy, but Gorbachev mistrusted the intentions of the US military.

During their fourth and final summit in Moscow in May 1988 President Reagan acknowledged that the Soviet Union was a different place and lifted his earlier charge of an 'evil empire'. He put glasnost to the test by speaking to ordinary Russians in Red Square and addressed the students of Moscow University, wishing them a 'new world of reconciliation, friendship and peace'.[9] In December 1988, as Reagan's presidency ended, Gorbachev enhanced his credentials as a peacemaker. In an address to the United Nations he renounced war, rescinded the Brezhnev Doctrine and consigned the Bolshevik Revolution to history as no longer relevant to the modern world. The Cold War was essentially over and in September 1989 Gorbachev cleared the way for an end to the arms race by removing his objection to SDI. Gorbachev could afford to ignore SDI as tests of the X-ray laser technology had failed. In addition, Congress had downgraded SDI funding and prohibited any tests in space. Gorbachev's commitment to peace was recognised in June 1990 with the award of the Nobel Peace Prize and *Time* magazine named him as 'Man of the Year'.

The logjam was broken and in July 1991 President Bush and Gorbachev signed a Strategic Arms Reduction Talk (START) treaty. The agreement cut strategic missiles by 50 per cent to a new joint level of 6000 warheads and 1600 strategic launchers. The end of the arms race was finally confirmed on 27th September 1991 when President Bush, as commander-in-chief of the US armed forces, 'stood down' the twenty-four-hour strategic alert status of the USAF. The USSR was no longer considered to be a military threat.

Gorbachev's approach to the deadlocked Mutual Balanced Force Reduction (MBFR) talks between the Warsaw Pact and NATO was equally dramatic. In April 1987 he stated his opposition to 'the division of the continent into military blocs'[10] and spoke of a 'common European home' and the need for closer East–West contacts. To demonstrate his commitment to European disarmament, Gorbachev announced to the United Nations in December 1988 unilateral cuts to the Warsaw Pact forces of 10 per cent, which meant the withdrawal of approximately 500,000 men and 10,000 tanks. The MBFR talks were wound up in February 1989 after sixteen years of sterile discussions, and were replaced by the Conventional Forces in Europe (CFE) talks of March 1989. Gorbachev's actions had broken the traditional suspicion of Soviet intentions and on 6th July 1990 NATO declared that the military confrontation was over. There was immediate agreement on a strict parity of conventional forces between the Warsaw Pact and NATO. In November 1950 the CFE Treaty specified the core military balance as 195,000 troops, 20,000 tanks and 6800 tactical aircraft. On 21st November 1990 the Conference for European Security and Co-operation issued a statement on behalf of the nations of Europe declaring that the Cold War was over.

Gorbachev also acted swiftly to end Western fears of Soviet expansionism and in April 1988 agreed to a Soviet withdrawal from Afghanistan. The final Soviet troops left Afghanistan on 21st February 1989 and Gorbachev also ended financial support to Nicaragua, Vietnam, Cambodia, Angola and Ethiopia. The factors that had prompted the renewal of the Cold War in 1979 – SS20 missiles, Afghanistan, Soviet expansionism and strategic imbalance – were all swept away.

Glasnost had transformed the Cold War and Gorbachev hoped that perestroika would equally transform the moribund Soviet economy and the somnolent CPSU. Having removed the heavy costs of the arms race, Gorbachev expected to modernise the Soviet Union and exploit the rich resources of the country to create a true economic super-power for the twenty-first century. The collapse of the USSR was not envisaged. Sakwa, reviewing Gorbachev's reforms as late as 1990, wrote, 'the USSR is placed to become perhaps the most dynamic economy of the twenty-first century'.[11] Gorbachev launched his reforms at the Twenty-seventh CPSU Party Congress of February 1986. The mood was extremely upbeat with the prediction, 'the economic capacity of the Soviet Union is to increase by 100% by the year 2000'.[12]

The only way was up. In the year of the seventieth anniversary of the 1917 revolution there was little to celebrate, with an economic growth rate of zero. The achievements of the CPSU were threadbare and glasnost placed its right to govern the state on public trial. Gorbachev admitted the failure of the Soviet economy in his book *Perestroika*, but equally promised to correct the deficiencies. The subsequent failure of his economic reforms intensified criticisms of the CPSU as the economy approached total collapse in 1988. Gorbachev retained his belief in the legitimacy of the CPSU and believed that the democratic reform of the Party would restore public confidence, but events in Eastern Europe switched control from top to bottom.

Glasnost offered Eastern Europe 'the right of every nation to choose its own path'.[13] In April 1989 Gorbachev informed the communist leaders of Eastern Europe that they must govern without Soviet sup-port, and in May 1989 Shevardnadze reinforced the point by stating, 'he could imagine no occasion in which Soviet troops might intervene in a Warsaw Pact county'.[14] The first test of the new freedom was in Hungary in May 1989 when border controls were ended. The Iron Curtain was breached and thousands of East Germans crossed the open border to freedom in West Germany. In June 1989 Poland elected a democratic Solidarity government and in swift succession the communist governments of Czechoslovakia, Bulgaria, East Germany and Romania all collapsed. Only in Romania was there resistance to change when President Ceauşescu attempted an army crackdown. The end was swift. He was publicly jeered as he gave a speech on 21st December 1989 and was executed alongside his wife four days later after an attempt to flee the country. The democratic revolution was symbolised most of all by the destruction of the Berlin Wall on 9th November 1989. On 12th September 1990 the Four Allied powers – the Soviet Union, the United States, Britain and France – finally ended their forty-five-year disagreement that had divided Germany and Europe, and agreed to the reunification of Germany. Glasnost had permitted free choice and the choice was democracy, but in the Soviet Union Gorbachev believed he could control events and 'unite socialism with democracy'.[15]

The West watched the disintegration of Eastern Europe in silence. It was a domestic affair. However, President Bush was criticised for inadequate leadership. He lacked the charisma of Gorbachev or Reagan and the *New York Times* savaged his speeches as 'flat and flimsy'.[16] The Polish Solidarity activist Adam Michnik more vividly accused him of 'sleepwalking through history'.[17]

Gorbachev remained extremely popular in the West but on May Day 1990 the jeers and boos of protesters forced him to withdraw from the traditional procession. The protests fragmented the CPSU and Soviet society. The most effective and sustained criticism arose from Boris Yeltsin, who after being sacked from the Politburo by Gorbachev in 1988 was elected president of the Republic of Russia in 1990. Yeltsin questioned the right of the CPSU to continue without a mandate from the people and promoted the independence and rights of Russia and the other fourteen republics. President Bush gave his support to Gorbachev at a meeting in Malta in December 1989 and ended up in the paradoxical situation of supporting the rule of the CPSU against the democratic demands of Yeltsin. Gorbachev represented stability whereas Yeltsin had the reputation of being impulsive and frequently drunk. However, much to Gorbachev's later irritation, the G7 summit of industrial leaders on 17th July 1991 refused financial support to assist the restructuring of the Soviet Union. There was to be no new

Marshall Plan for the Soviet economy, which was regarded as a financial black hole.

Gorbachev veered sharply right and left in his attempts to steer through the crisis but simply alienated support in both camps. In November 1990 he invited Soviet hard-liners into government and provoked the resignation of Eduard Shevardnadze, who warned that a return to dictatorship was imminent. The crackdown on dissent in Lithuania in January 1991 and army patrols of Moscow appeared to bear out his words. In June 1991 a public poll showed that Gorbachev's approval rating was only 10 per cent – a decline from 52 per cent in 1989. He attempted to restore his democratic credentials in July 1991 by announcing plans for all government posts to be elected, something that immediately threatened the position of the Soviet hard-liners.

At 5 p.m. on 18th August 1991 Gorbachev was disturbed while on holiday at his dacha in Foros in the Crimea by representatives of his cabinet: 'they had come with an ultimatum'.[18] He was placed under house arrest while his own prime minister, Valentin Pavlov, attempted to seize control and restore the authority of the CPSU. The coup was half-hearted and the plotters failed to remove key opponents such as Yeltsin, who immediately rallied the people of Moscow to defend democracy. The attitude of the army was crucial, and the Soviet Army refused to storm the Russian Parliament to arrest Yeltsin, and the coup fizzled out on 21st August 1991.

It proved to be the downfall of the CPSU as Yeltsin launched a counter-coup and passed a decree in the Russian Parliament to ban the CPSU. This ban was then extended throughout the USSR on 29th August by the Supreme Soviet. Gorbachev appeared before the Russian Parliament and in a televised speech attempted to announce an investigation, but he was humiliated by jeers and catcalls. Yeltsin thrust the names of the coup leaders in front of an obviously shaken Gorbachev. Outside in the streets people overturned statues of Lenin. The role of the CPSU as the 'vanguard of the people' was over.

The future of the USSR was still unclear and Gorbachev hoped that the fifteen republics would agree to co-operate in a new democratic USSR with himself remaining as president, pending elections. The attitude of Ukraine, the second most populous of the fifteen republics after Russia was crucial. In 1984, while Gorbachev was on his first visit to London, a protester had evaded a security cordon to shout, 'Freedom for the Ukraine.'[19] The words returned to haunt Gorbachev as on 1st December 1991 the Ukrainian people voted for independence in a referendum. The USSR was rejected. Glasnost had permitted the people to speak and they had spoken. On 8th December 1991, eleven of the fifteen republics formed the Commonwealth of Independent States (CIS) and 31st December 1991 was declared the transition date from the USSR.

Yeltsin was impatient for the end and to Gorbachev's anger insisted that he vacate the Kremlin on Christmas Day 1991. In his memoirs Gorbachev noted that Yeltsin personally 'supervised my expulsion from the Kremlin'[20] and subsequently occupied his office and held a party. Other than the lowering of the Hammer and Sickle and the raising of the Russian flag above the Kremlin there was no ceremony to mark the passing of communism.

Today, Lenin, alone in his mausoleum, remains the last reminder of the communist dream of a just, more equal way of life, and the reluctance to bury him is the reluctance to bury the dream of what might have been.

Glasnost exploded the myths of Cold War confrontation and the 'triumphs' of communism and, more in sorrow than anger, the USSR imploded.

Questions

1. How far did ordinary people dictate the pace of change in the USSR?
2. To what extent did the pressure of SDI and the arms build-up force an end to the Cold War?

ANALYSIS (2): WHO WON THE COLD WAR?

The core of the Cold War dispute was a struggle between totalitarianism and democracy, and democracy won. The confrontation between the Soviet Union and the United States ended in 1988 with a joint cessation not a US victory and it was the internal battle for democracy from 1989 to 1991 that finally destroyed the Soviet Union. Gorbachev recognised that totalitarianism had failed the Soviet Union and he sought to fuse democracy with socialism in a bid to transform his country into an economic superpower for the twenty-first century.

The acceptance of democracy immediately removed the ideological confrontation with the West. Gorbachev also recognised the benefits of private enterprise and hoped for trade and joint ventures with Western companies to remodel the Soviet economy. This involved an admission of the failure of the Soviet planned economy but it was an admission Gorbachev freely made in his book *Perestroika*. In these circumstances the Cold War was an unnecessary barrier to co-operation. Consequently, Gorbachev offered President Reagan first a truce and then a cessation of the arms race.

The Soviet Union did not surrender to the United States from 1985 to 1988 but established strict military equality and sought partnership for the future. It was to Reagan's credit that he accepted a cessation and resisted the urgings of the defence lobby to deny disarmament and increase the pressure to force outright capitulation. However, it took substantial military concessions from Gorbachev along with the withdrawal from Afghanistan, Eastern Europe and the Third World finally to undercut the 'Soviet menace' objections of the US hawks.

The new Soviet Union was presented to the world in December 1988 in Gorbachev's United Nations speech after President Reagan had already given it his blessing and acknowledged that the 'evil empire' was gone during the Moscow Summit of May 1988.

The collapse of the Soviet Union was entirely unforeseen by either Gorbachev or the Western world. The *raison d'être* of any government is to feed the people and Gorbachev neglected the lesson of 1917. In 1990 the empty shops fed protest. The party of the people had to accept that the people did not want it and ultimately they voted the USSR out of existence. Glasnost defeated the Soviet Union.

The end of the Cold War coincided with Reagan's military challenge to the Soviet Union and this has promoted the theory that Reagan won the Cold War. This claim is undermined by the fact that Yuri Andropov absorbed Reagan's challenge between 1982 and 1984 and refused to make any concessions in the arms race. Reagan also promised to share SDI technology with the Soviet Union in an 'open labs' policy, which contradicts the theory of a plan to force the Soviet Union into overspend. There was a defence lobby at the heart of Reagan's administration who recommended breaking the Soviet economy but it was a lobby, not a strategy. The Soviet Union was in crisis before Reagan became president and it was in response to this internal crisis that Gorbachev acted to end the Cold War.

This conclusion was largely confirmed by some of the main Cold War-era leaders in October 1995. President Bush invited the ex-Cold War leaders to Colorado Springs as a fundraising venture for the Bush Presidential Library. In attendance were Margaret Thatcher, François Mitterrand, Mikhail Gorbachev and Brian Mulroney. Ill health prevented the attendance of Ronald Reagan.

Only Margaret Thatcher expressed the view that the Strategic Defense Initiative (SDI) and the arms race had forced the Soviet Union to end the Cold War. Gorbachev, with support from Mitterrand and Mulroney, emphasised the internal collapse of the Soviet Union and said that events had simply spiralled out of political control. President Bush confirmed that the West remained on the sidelines as the USSR collapsed from 1989 to 1991. The US strategy was to avoid being overly triumphant and to support Gorbachev to ward off the possible rise of a hard-line military dictatorship.

In 1953 President Truman made an uncannily accurate forecast of events. It is worth quoting at length the words of his last broadcast to the nation as president of the United States on 15th January 1953:

> As the free world grows stronger, more united, more attractive to men on both sides of the Iron Curtain and as the Soviet hopes for easy expansion are blocked – then there will have to come a time of change in the Soviet world. Nobody can say for sure when that is going to be or exactly how it will come about – whether by revolution or trouble in satellite states or by changes inside the Kremlin. Whether the communist rulers shift their policies of their own free will – or whether the changes come about in some other way – I have not a doubt in the world that a change will occur. I have a deep abiding faith in the destiny of free men. With patience and courage we shall some day move into a new era.[21]

The new era finally dawned in 1991 after a forty-five-year long battle of attrition and a victory for Truman's policy of containment. It did take time and patience, but ultimately it was communism rather than capitalism that contained the internal dialectic. Communism defeated itself.

Questions

1. Were the members of the Reagan administration spectators of a Soviet domestic crisis or the instigators of a deliberate strategy to undermine the Soviet Union?
2. To what extent did Gorbachev have choices, or had he no alternative but to end the Cold War?

SOURCES

1. THE TRANSITION TO AGREEMENT

Source A: commitment to SDI.

President Reagan recorded in his memoirs his commitment to SDI and the tension between Secretary of State Shultz and Secretary of Defense Weinberger.

Cap Weinberger strongly believed we should resist all Soviet efforts to limit research on the Strategic Defense Initiative . . . Cap said what made him especially angry was that the Russians were whining about our research on the SDI while they had been conducting similar research of their own for more than twenty years. Even though I entirely agreed with Cap on this one, I sometimes had to ask him to mute his most critical public comments about the Soviets and turned him down when he wanted me to speak more harshly toward the Russians than I thought prudent at a time we were trying to improve relations with them. During this period Cap and George Shultz were often at odds over how to deal with the Russians . . . One thing I do know is I won't trade our SDI off for some Soviet offer of weapon reductions . . . got fitted for a new bullet-proof raincoat and went home.

Source B: Reagan at the Berlin Wall.

On 12th June 1987 President Reagan visited Berlin and recorded his uncertainties about Gorbachev's reforms.

We hear much from Moscow about a new policy of reform and openness . . . Are these the beginnings of profound changes in the Soviet State? Or are they token gestures intended to raise false hopes in the West, or to strengthen the Soviet system without changing it? . . . There is one sign the Soviets can make that would be unmistakable, that would advance dramatically the cause of freedom and peace. General Secretary Gorbachev, if you seek peace, if you seek prosperity for the Soviet Union and Eastern Europe, if you seek liberalisation: Come here to this gate! Mr Gorbachev, open this gate! Mr Gorbachev, tear down this wall!

Source C: Washington Summit.

On 8th September 1987 General Secretary Gorbachev welcomed the signing of the Intermediate Nuclear Forces Treaty with President Reagan which removed all nuclear missiles from Europe.

Mankind has come to realise that it has had enough wars and that it is time to put an end to them for good . . . The world of today is not a monopoly of one nation or group of nations whatever their power. The world is a common home and a common cause for a plurality of individuals . . . To put it in simple human language, what we have achieved is both in Russian and English the revival of hope.

Source D: President Reagan at Moscow University.

On 31st May 1988, while attending the Moscow Summit, President Reagan addressed the students of Moscow University.

Your generation is living in one of the most exciting, hopeful times in Soviet history. It is a time when the first breath of freedom stirs the air and the heart beats to the accelerated rhythm of hope, when the accumulated spiritual energies of a long silence yearn to break free . . . We do not know what the conclusion will be of this journey, but we're hopeful that the promise of reform will be fulfilled . . . We may be allowed to hope that the marvellous sound of a new openness will keep rising through, ringing through, leading to a new world of reconciliation, friendship and peace. Thank you all very much and *da blagoslovit vas gospod* – God bless you.

Questions

1. With reference to Source A, what evidence does President Reagan provide of his aims?
2. What insight do Sources A and B provide of the debate over policy within the Reagan administration towards the Soviet Union?
*3. How far do Gorbachev (Source C) and President Reagan (Source D) express similar sentiments?
4. Considering all four sources and your own knowledge, answer the following question: Why did President Reagan end his challenge to the Soviet Union in 1988?

Worked answer

*3. Although President Reagan and General Secretary Gorbachev were separated by many years of Cold War hostility, the sentiments they express in Sources C and D are remarkably similar. Both men were speaking for public consumption: Gorbachev at the Washington Summit of 1987 after the breakthrough of the INF Treaty and Reagan to the students of Moscow University in 1988 during the Moscow

Summit. The sentiments that both leaders share are of peace and goodwill and the mutual acceptance that the Cold War is over. Gorbachev, in Source C, refers to mankind having had 'enough wars' and to the world as a 'common home', with the implication of a new future of equality between nations. Reagan shares this sentiment in Source D with the words, 'new world of reconciliation' and sees a future that heralds 'the promise of reform'. Both leaders express the sentiment of hope. Gorbachev speaks of the 'revival of hope' and Reagan speaks of 'hopeful times' in an overall impression of the dawn of a new age.

SOURCES

2. THE COLLAPSE OF THE SOVIET UNION

Source E: end of Communist rule.

On 24th August 1991 the *Daily Telegraph* newspaper carried the following account of events in the Russian Parliament after the suppression of the Communist Party's coup.

The humiliation of President Gorbachev was completed yesterday by Mr Boris Yeltsin and his Russian deputies in the building where they led the resistance to the Soviet coup. A hesitant and flustered Soviet leader who has failed to grasp the tidal wave of revolutionary sentiment since his release from captivity on Wednesday was shouted down as he defended the Communist Party and urged the Russian Parliament to show restraint . . . He will not forget the experience which was televised live to tens of millions of viewers. At one point Mr Yeltsin strode over from his seat at the centre of the stage to Mr Gorbachev who was standing at a lectern, and towering above him gave him a document to read out in public . . . It was the minutes of a cabinet meeting on Monday, the first day of the coup, showing that virtually all Mr Gorbachev's ministers had betrayed him . . . 'On a lighter note, shall we now sign a decree suspending the activities of the Russian Communist Party? I will now sign it,' Mr Yeltsin said grandiosely, his voice booming. He began putting pen to paper. 'Boris Nikolayevich, Boris Nikolayevich,' Mr Gorbachev beseeched him. Mr Yeltsin cast a cursory glance at his long-time adversary, smiled and signed. Deputies rose in unison, clapping and cheering.

Source F: end of the USSR.

On 27th August 1991 the *Daily Telegraph* reported upon the political break-up of the USSR.

President Gorbachev bowed to the inevitable yesterday and accepted that the Baltic States and the other republics could leave the Soviet Union almost immediately. With the Union disintegrating around him, he told a special session of the Federal Parliament in Moscow that he had not abandoned hope that there would be some kind of continuing loose association involving its fifteen republics.

Source G: Gorbachev's last speech.

On 25th December 1991, immediately before he left the Kremlin for the last time, President Gorbachev delivered the following televised speech to the Russian people.

Fate had decided that when I became head of state, it was already obvious that there was something wrong in this country. We had plenty of everything: land, oil, gas and other natural resources and God has also endowed us with intellect and talent – yet we lived much worse than people in other industrialised countries and the gap was constantly widening. The reason was apparent even then – our society was stifled in the grip of a bureaucratic command system. Doomed to serve ideology and bear the heavy burden of the arms race, it was strained to the utmost . . . an end has been put to the arms race and the insane militarisation of our county which crippled our economy, distorted our thinking and undermined our morals. The threat of a world war is no more.

Source H: a victory for democracy.

On 6th May 1992, as president of the Green Cross International organisation, Gorbachev made a speech at Fulton, Missouri, where Churchill's Iron Curtain speech announced the Cold War in 1946.

In the major centres of world politics the choice it would seem has today been made in favour of peace, co-operation, interaction and common security. And in pushing forward to a new civilisation we should under no circumstances again make the intellectual and consequently political error of interpreting victory in the Cold War narrowly as a victory for oneself, one's own way of life, for one's own values and merits. This was a victory over a scheme for the development of humanity which was becoming slowly congealed and leading us to destruction. It was a shattering of the vicious circle into which we had driven ourselves. This was altogether a victory for common sense, reason, democracy and common human values.

Questions

1. With reference to Source E, comment on why President Gorbachev was unable to prevent the banning of the CPSU?
*2. How does the language and tone of Source F indicate that Gorbachev was reluctant to relinquish control?
3. In what ways do Sources E and F demonstrate the failure of Gorbachev's reforms of the CPSU?
4. Why, according to the evidence of Sources G and H, did the Soviet Union collapse?
5. With reference to Sources F to H and to your own knowledge, answer the following question: How far did internal rather than external forces cause the collapse of the Soviet Union?

Worked answer

*2. The language and tone of Source F conveys the impression of Gorbachev at bay and unable to control events. The words, 'bowed to the inevitable' clearly indicate reluctance on Gorbachev's part to accept the decision of the Soviet republics to leave the Soviet Union, and the tone suggests a hope that they might reconsider. This is reinforced by the statement that Gorbachev had 'not abandoned hope' and confirms a desire to restore some measure of control over events. Overall, the impression given is of a leader saddened by events and hoping to salvage some form of control, perhaps in the form of a 'loose association' of the newly independent republics.

NOTES

1. EMERGENCE OF THE COLD WAR

1. Paterson, 1988, p. 52.
2. Carr, 1966, p. 123.
3. Bullock, 1962, p. 354.
4. Yergin, 1978, p. 19.
5. Feis, 1970, p. 49.
6. McCauley, 1983, p. 114.
7. Deutscher, 1961, p. 328.
8. Bullock, 1991, p. 667.
9. Ibid., p. 684.
10. Paterson, op. cit., p. 52.
11. McCauley, op. cit., p. 109.
12. Higgins, 1977, p. 36.
13. Shaw, 1998, p. 75.
14. Gaddis, 1997, p. 294.
15. Zubok and Pleshakov, 1996, pp. 74, 276.
16. Taylor, 1978, p. 146.
17. Volkogonov, 1991, p. 484.
18. Deutscher, op. cit., p. 478.
19. Lee, 1990, p. 76.
20. Deutscher, op. cit., p. 475.
21. Khrushchev, 1971, p. 197.
22. Volkogonov, op. cit., p. 486.
23. McCauley, op. cit., p. 39.
24. Gilbert, 1992, p. 820.
25. McCauley, op. cit., p. 42.
26. Ibid., p. 44.
27. Gilbert, op. cit., p. 857.
Source A: Rayner, 1992, p. 7.
Source B: McCauley, op. cit., p. 115.
Source C: Ibid., p. 105.

Source D: Ibid., p. 94.
Source E: Ibid., p. 113.
Source F: Khrushchev, op. cit., p. 196.
Source G: Volkogonov, op. cit., p. 489.
Source H: Mee, 1975, p. 101.

2. CONFRONTATION

1. Volkogonov, op. cit., p. 504.
2. Ulam, 1973, p. 641.
3. Gaddis, 1987, p. 28.
4. Zubok and Pleshakov, op. cit., p. 40.
5. Khrushchev, op. cit., p. 357.
6. Bullock, 1991, op. cit., p. 961.
7. Zubok and Pleshakov, op. cit., p. 39.
8. Truman, 1965, p. 119.
9. Dunbabin, 1994, p. 15.
10. McCullough, 1992, p. 486.
11. Paterson, op. cit., p. 51.
12. Mooney and Brown, 1979, p. 12.
13. Paterson, op. cit., p. 116.
14. Ulam, op. cit., p. 659.
15. Leffler and Painter, 1994, p. 55.
16. Gaddis, 1987, op. cit., p. 46.
17. McCullough, op. cit., p. 772.
18. Walker, 1993, p. 66.
19. Ulam, op. cit., p. 697.
20. McCullough, op. cit., p. 772.
21. Ibid., p. 775.
22. Zubok and Pleshakov, op. cit., p. 54.
23. Volkogonov, op. cit., p. 524.
24. Medvedev, 1982, p. 88.
25. Walker, op. cit., p. 29.
26. Gaddis, 1987, op. cit., p. 53.
27. Commager, 1973, p. 503.
28. Gaddis, 1987, op. cit., p. 53.
29. Dunbabin, op. cit., p. 62.
30. Truman, op. cit., p. 605.
31. Ibid., p. 606.
32. McCauley, op. cit., p. 132.
33. Gaddis, 1987, op. cit., p. 38.
34. Truman, op. cit., p. 613.
35. McCullough, op. cit., p. 514.
36. Ibid., p. 517.
37. Truman, op. cit., p. 129.

38. Gaddis, 1982, p. 41.
39. Yergin, op. cit., p. 294.
40. Bullock, 1991, op. cit., p. 294.
41. Truman, op. cit., p. 129.
42. McCullough, op. cit., p. 563.
43. Ball, 1998, p. 57.
44. Gaddis, 1982, op. cit., p. 97.
45. Walker, op. cit., p. 77.
46. Commager, op. cit., p. 567.
47. McCullough, op. cit., p. 911.
48. Volkogonov, op. cit., p. 533.
49. McCullough, op. cit., p. 764.
50. Walker, op. cit., p. 69.
Source A: Rayner, op. cit., p. 15.
Source B: McCauley, op. cit., p. 100.
Source C: Commager, op. cit., p. 525.
Source D: Rayner, op. cit., p. 17.
Source E: Truman, op. cit., p. 157.
Source F: Khrushchev, op. cit., p. 416.
Source G: Ibid., p. 333.
Source H: Commager, op. cit., p. 567.

3. PEACEFUL COEXISTENCE

1. Dunbabin, op. cit., p. 126.
2. Zubok and Pleshakov, op. cit., p. 155.
3. Gilbert, op. cit., p. 921.
4. Mooney and Brown, op. cit., p. 81.
5. Dougherty and Pfaltzgraff, 1986, p. 101.
6. Dunbabin, op. cit., p. 130.
7. Eden, 1960, p. 300.
8. Khrushchev, op. cit., p. 361.
9. Ball, op. cit., p. 77.
10. Eden, op. cit., p. 306.
11. Higgins, op. cit., p. 94.
12. McCauley, 1987, p. 182.
13. Commager, op. cit., p. 622.
14. Paterson, op. cit., p. 139.
15. Brown and Mooney, 1976, p. 71.
16. Khrushchev, op. cit., p. 361.
17. Ibid., p. 434.
18. Walker, op. cit., p. 127.
19. Mooney and Brown, op. cit., p. 75.
20. Gaddis, 1982, op. cit., p. 138.
21. Ibid., p. 149.

22. Commager, op. cit., p. 591.
23. Dunbabin, op. cit., p. 135.
24. Walker, op. cit., p. 129.
25. Ibid., p. 127.
26. Khrushchev, op. cit., p. 467.
27. Ibid.
28. Paterson, op. cit., p. 165.
29. Ibid., p. 181.
30. Walker, op. cit., p. 114.
31. Commager, op. cit., p. 653.
Source A: Eden, op. cit., p. 306.
Source B: Khrushchev, op. cit., p. 363.
Source C: Commager, op. cit., p. 590.
Source D: Khrushchev, op. cit., p. 476.
Source E: Ibid., p. 434.
Source F: Commager, op. cit., p. 597.
Source G: Ibid., p. 648.
Source H: Ibid., p. 649.

4. THE MISSILE RACE

1. Leffler and Painter, op. cit., p. 100.
2. Clark, 1980, p. 228.
3. Khrushchev, op. cit., p. 471.
4. Ibid., p. 371.
5. Ibid., p. 368.
6. Zubok and Pleshakov, op. cit., p. 193.
7. Khrushchev, op. cit., p. 472.
8. Commager, op. cit., p. 655.
9. Ibid., p. 596.
10. Sorensen, 1965, p. 678.
11. Walker, op. cit., p. 170.
12. Khrushchev, op. cit., p. 455.
13. Sorensen, op. cit., p. 681.
14. Schlesinger, 1965, p. 705.
15. Walker, op. cit., p. 178.
16. Sorensen, op. cit., p. 717.
17. Khrushchev, op. cit., p. 462.
Source A: Keesings, 1957–58, vol. XI, p. 15,791.
Source B: Ibid., p. 15,861.
Source C: Ibid., 1961, vol. XIII, p. 17,849.
Source D: Young, 1993, p. 313.
Sources E to K: *The Times* – see text for dates.

5. DÉTENTE

1. Commager, op. cit., p. 677.
2. Ball, op. cit., p. 130.
3. Nixon, 1978, p. 366.
4. Ibid., p. 395.
5. Garthoff, 1985, p. 30.
6. Nixon, op. cit., p. 580.
7. Garthoff, op. cit., p. 77.
8. Ibid., p. 129.
9. Arbatov, 1983, p. 69.
10. Kissinger, 1994, p. 736.
11. Ibid.
Source A: Commager, op. cit., p. 676.
Source B: Keesings, 1971–72, vol. XVIII, p. 25,093.
Source C: Nixon, op. cit., p. 577.
Source D: Zagladin, 1984, p. 24.
Source E: Ibid., p. 37.
Source F: Keesings, 1973, vol. XIX, p. 25,997.
Source G: Ibid., 1966, vol. XV, p. 21,498.
Source H: Ibid., p. 21,500.

6. DISARMAMENT

1. Nixon, op. cit., p. 416.
2. Keesings, 1973, vol. XIX, p. 25,045.
3. Nixon, op. cit., p. 524.
4. Garthoff, op. cit., p. 194.
5. Ambrose, 1989, p. 440.
6. Nixon, op. cit., p. 1036.
7. Nekrasov, 1984, p. 62.
8. Ibid., p. 64.
9. Rayner, 1992, p. 74.
10. Zagladin, op. cit., p. 79.
11. Mooney and Brown, op. cit., p. 262.
12. Zagladin, op. cit., p. 110.
13. Lee, 1981, p. 15.
Source A: Commager, op. cit., p. 772.
Source B: Nixon, op. cit., p. 1032.
Source C: http://carterlibrary.galileo.peachnet.edu.
Source D: Zagladin, op. cit., p. 80.
Source E: http://www.nato.int.
Source F: Zagladin, op. cit., p. 110.
Source G: http://www.nato.int.
Source H: Lee, op. cit., p. 15.

7. EVIL EMPIRE

1. Haftendom and Schissler, 1988, p. 4.
2. Reagan, 1990, p. 219.
3. M. Walker, op. cit., p. 219.
4. Reagan, op. cit., p. 265.
5. Haftendom and Schissler, op. cit., p. 7.
6. Reagan, op. cit., p. 574.
7. Gorbachev, 1987, p. 236.
8. Reagan, op. cit., p. 556.
9. Ibid., p. 555.
10. Powaski, 1998, p. 250.
11. Arbatov, op. cit., p. 85.
12. Reagan, op. cit., p. 570.
13. Hill, 1990, p. 211.
14. Haftendom and Schissler, op. cit., p. 152.
15. Ibid.
16. Medvedev, 1984, p. 196.
17. Westwood, 1993, p. 471.
18. Andropov, 1983, p. 13.
19. Novosti, 1967, p. 19.
20. Medvedev, 1984, p. 134.
21. Novosti, op. cit., p. 4.
22. Novosti, 1987, p. 63.
23. Novosti, 1967, op. cit., p. 13.
24. Gerasimov, 1986, p. 56.
25. Ibid., p. 4.
26. Sakwa, 1990, p. 1.
27. Schmidt-Hauer, 1986, p. 101.
28. Ibid., p. 115.
29. Gorbachev, op. cit., p. 225.
Source A: Reagan, op. cit., p. 266.
Source B: http://sunsite.unc.edu/lia/president/reagan.html.
Source C: Andropov, op. cit., p. 30.
Source D: Reagan, op. cit., p. 599.
Source E: Gerasimov, op. cit., p. 42.
Source F: Novosti, 1987, p. 10.
Source G: *Guardian*, 12th September 1987.
Source H: *The Economist*, 21st November 1987.

8. GLASNOST

1. Gorbachev, op. cit., p. 17.
2. Ibid., p. 12.
3. Ibid., p. 142.

4. Reagan, op. cit., p. 703.
5. Gorbachev, op. cit., p. 234.
6. Powaski, op. cit., p. 250.
7. Gorbachev, op. cit., p. 220.
8. Reagan, op. cit., p. 675.
9. Ibid., p. 714.
10. Sakwa, op. cit. p. 337.
11. Ibid., p. 313.
12. Gerasimov, op. cit., p. 41.
13. Gorbachev, op. cit., p. 143.
14. Sakwa, op. cit., p. 343.
15. Gorbachev, op. cit., p. 35.
16. Boyle, 1993, p. 228.
17. R. Walker, 1993, p. 311.
18. Gorbachev, 1996, p. 631.
19. Schmidt-Hauer, op. cit., p. 6.
20. Gorbachev, 1996, op. cit., p. 671.
21. McCullough, op. cit., p. 919.
Source A: Reagan, op. cit., p. 628.
Source B: Ibid., p. 683.
Source C: Gorbachev, 1996, op. cit., p. 449.
Source D: http://sunsite.unc.edu/lia/president/reagan.html.
Source E: *Daily Telegraph*, 24th August 1991.
Source F: Ibid., 27th August 1991.
Source G: Gorbachev, 1996, op. cit., p. 25.
Source H: http://www.gci.ch/.

BIBLIOGRAPHY

SELECTED WORKS

There is an extensive range of literature on the Cold War, but perhaps the best starting point is with the aims, opinions and attitudes of the principal participants. The 'Big Three' are brought to life by: Isaac Deutscher: *Stalin: A Political Biography* (Pelican 1966), given a Russian perspective by Dmitri Volkogonov: *Stalin: Triumph and Tragedy* (Weidenfeld and Nicolson 1991); Martin Gilbert: *Churchill: A Life* (Heinemann 1992); and Robert E. Sherwood: *Roosevelt and Hopkins* (Harper and Bros. 1950). A useful three in one is provided by: Herbert Feis: *Churchill, Roosevelt, Stalin* (Oxford University Press 1957).

For the immediate development of the Cold War: George F. Kennan: *Memoirs 1925–50* (Little, Brown 1967); Harry S Truman: *Memoirs Vol. 1: 1945, Year of Decisions* (Signet 1965); Harry S Truman: *Memoirs Vol. 2: 1946–1952, Years of Trial and Hope* (Signet 1965); Nikita Khrushchev (trans. Strobe Talbott): *Khrushchev Remembers* (Sphere 1971).

The later ups and downs may be surveyed through: Stephen E. Ambrose: *Eisenhower, The President* (Allen and Unwin 1983); Theodore C. Sorensen: *Kennedy* (Hodder and Stoughton 1965); Richard Nixon: *The Memoirs of Richard Nixon* (Book Club Associates 1978); Henry Kissinger: *Diplomacy* (Simon and Schuster 1994); Andrei Gromyko: *Memoirs* (Doubleday 1989); Ronald Reagan: *Ronald Reagan: An American Life, the Autobiography* (Hutchinson 1990); Mikhail Gorbachev: *Memoirs* (Transworld 1996).

For comprehensive, readable overviews try: Martin Walker: *The Cold War* (Fourth Estate 1993); S.J. Ball: *The Cold War* (Hodder Headline 1998); J.P.D. Dunbabin: *The Cold War: The Great Powers and Their Allies* (Longman 1994); Ronald E. Powaski: *The Cold War* (Oxford University Press 1998); Joseph Smith: *The Cold War 1945–91* (Blackwell 1998).

To explore some of the key issues in more depth try: Vladislav Zubok and Constantine Pleshakov: *Inside the Kremlin's Cold War: From Stalin to Khrushchev* (Harvard University Press 1996); John Lewis Gaddis: *We Now Know: Rethinking Cold War History* (Oxford University Press 1997); Mikhail Gorbachev: *Perestroika* (William Collins & Sons 1987); Daniel Yergin: *Shattered Peace: The Origins Of The Cold War and the National Security State* (Penguin 1990); Peter G. Boyle: *American–Soviet Relations* (Routledge 1993); Melvyn P. Leffler: *A Preponderance of Power: National Security, the Truman Administration and the Cold War* (Stanford 1992); Melvyn Leffler and David Painter (eds): *Origins of the Cold War* (Routledge 1994); Martin McCauley: *The Origins of the Cold War, 1941–49* (Longman 1983); Walter LaFeber: *America, Russia and the Cold War 1945–1990*, sixth edition (McGraw Hill 1991); Thomas G. Paterson: *Meeting the Communist Threat: America's Cold War History* (Oxford University Press 1988); Raymond L. Garthoff: *Detente and Confrontation: American–Soviet Relations from Nixon to Reagan* (Brookings Institution 1985).

REFERENCES

Andropov, Yuri, *Our Aim is to Preserve Peace*, Novosti, 1983.

Ambrose, Stephen E., *Nixon, the Triumph of a Politician 1962–1972*, Simon and Schuster, 1989.

Arbatov, Georgi, *Cold War or Detente*, Zed Books, 1983.

Ball, S.J., *The Cold War*, Hodder Headline, 1998.

Boyle, Peter G., *American–Soviet Relations*, Routledge, 1993.

Brown, Colin and Mooney, Peter, *Cold War to Detente*, Heinemann, 1976.

Bullock, Alan, *Hitler: A Study in Tyranny*, Pelican, 1962.

Bullock, Alan, *Hitler and Stalin: Parallel Lives*, HarperCollins, 1991.

Carr, E.H., *The Bolshevik Revolution, Vol. 1: 1917–1923*, Pelican, 1966.

Clark, Ronald W., *The Greatest Power on Earth: The Story of Nuclear Fission*, Sidgwick and Jackson, 1980.

Commager, Henry Steele, *Documents of American History Vol. II: Since 1898*, ninth edition, Prentice-Hall, 1973.

Deutscher, Isaac, *Stalin: A Political Biography*, Oxford University Press, 1961.

Dougherty, James and Pfaltzgraff, Robert L. jr, *American Foreign Policy: FDR to Reagan*, Harper and Row, 1986.

Dunbabin, J.P.D., *The Cold War: The Great Powers and Their Allies*, Longman, 1994.

Eden, Anthony Sir, *Full Circle: The Memoirs of Sir Anthony Eden*, Cassell, 1960.

Feis, Herbert, *From Trust to Terror: The Onset of the Cold War 1945–80*, Anthony Blond, 1970.

Gaddis, John Lewis, *Strategies of Containment: A Critical Appraisal of Postwar American National Security Policy*, Oxford University Press, 1982.

Gaddis, John Lewis, *The Long Peace: Inquiries into the History of the Cold War*, Oxford University Press, 1987.

Gaddis, John Lewis, *We Now Know*, Clarendon Press, 1997.

Garthoff, Raymond L., *Detente and Confrontation: American–Soviet Relations from Nixon to Reagan*, Brookings Institution, 1985.

Gerasimov, Gennadi (ed.), *The Soviet Course: Peace and Renovation*, Novosti Press, 1986.

Gilbert, Martin, *Churchill: A Life*, Heinemann, 1992.

Gorbachev, Mikhail, *Perestroika*, William Collins & Sons, 1987.

Gorbachev, Mikhail, *Memoirs*, Transworld, 1996.

Haftendom, Helga and Schissler, Jakob (eds), *The Reagan Administration: A Reconstruction of American Strength*, Walter de Gruyter, 1988.

Higgins, Hugh, *The Cold War*, Heinemann, first published 1974, this edn 1977.

Hill, Dilys M. (ed.), *The Reagan Presidency*, Macmillan Press, 1990.

Keesings Contemporary Archives, CIRCA Reference, Cartermill International 1996.

Kennan, George, *Russia and the West*, Hutchinson, 1961.

Kennan, George, *Memoirs, 1950–1963*, Hutchinson, 1972.

Kennedy, Robert, *Thirteen Days: A Memoir of the Cuban Missile Crisis*, W.W. Norton, 1969.

Khrushchev, Nikita (trans. Strobe Talbott), *Khrushchev Remembers*, Sphere, 1971.

Kissinger, Henry, *Diplomacy*, Simon and Schuster, 1994.

Kort, Michael, *The Soviet Colossus: A History of the USSR since 1965*, Routledge, 1992.

Lee, Christopher, *The Final Decade*, Hamish Hamilton, 1981.

Lee, Stephen J., *The European Dictatorships*, Routledge, 1990.

Leffler, Melvyn and Painter, David (eds), *Origins of the Cold War*, Routledge, 1994.

McCauley, Martin, *The Soviet Union since 1917*, Longman, 1981.

McCauley, Martin, *Origins of the Cold War, 1941–49*, Longman, 1983.

McCauley, Martin (ed.), *Khrushchev and Khrushchevism*, Macmillan, 1987.

McCauley, Martin, *The Khrushchev Era, 1953–1964*, Longman, 1995.

McCullough, David, *Truman*, Simon and Schuster, 1992.

Medvedev, Roy, *Khrushchev*, Blackwell, 1982.

Medvedev, Zhores, *Andropov: His Life and Death*, Basil Blackwell, 1984.

Mee, Charles L. jr, *Meeting at Potsdam*, André Deutsch, 1975.

Mooney, Peter J., *The Soviet Superpower*, Heinemann, 1982.

Mooney, Peter J. and Brown, Colin, *Truman to Carter*, Edward Arnold, 1979.

Nekrasov, Vadim, *The Roots of European Security*, Novosti Press, 1984.

Nixon, Richard, *The Memoirs of Richard Nixon*, Book Club Associates, 1978.

Novosti Press, *The Soviet Union 1917–1967*, 1967.

Novosti Press, *The Soviet Yearbook 1987*, 1987.

Paterson, Thomas G., *Meeting the Communist Threat, Truman to Reagan*, Oxford University Press, 1988.

Powaski, Ronald E., *The Cold War*, Oxford University Press, 1998.

Rayner, E.G., *The Cold War*, Hodder and Stoughton, 1992.

Reagan, Ronald, *Ronald Reagan: An American Life, the Autobiography*, Hutchinson, 1990.

Sakwa, Richard, *Gorbachev and His Reforms 1985–1990*, Simon and Schuster, 1990.

Schlesinger, Arthur M. jr, *A Thousand Days: John F. Kennedy in the White House*, Fawcett Cress, 1965.

Schmidt-Hauer, Christian, *Gorbachev: The Path to Power*, Tauris & Co., 1986.

Shaw, Tony, 'The British Popular Press and the Early Cold War', *Journal of the Historical Association*, Vol. 83, No. 269, 1998, pp. 75–78.

Smith, Joseph, *The Cold War 1945–91*, Historical Association, Blackwell, 1998.

Sorensen, Theodore C., *Kennedy*, Hodder and Stoughton, 1965.

Taylor, A.J.P., *The War Lords*, Hamish Hamilton, 1978.

Truman, Harry S, *Memoirs Vol. 1: 1945, Year of Decisions*, Signet, 1965.

Truman, Harry S, *Memoirs Vol. 2: 1946–1952, Years of Trial and Hope*, Signet, 1965.

Ulam, Adam B., *Stalin: The Man and His Era*, Viking Press, 1973.

Volkogonov, Dmitri, *Stalin: Triumph and Tragedy*, Weidenfeld and Nicolson, 1991.

Walker, Martin, *The Cold War*, Fourth Estate, 1993.

Westwood, J.N., *Endurance and Endeavour: Russian History 1812–1992*, Oxford University Press, 1993.

Yergin, Daniel, *The Shattered Peace: The Origins of the Cold War and the National Security State*, André Deutsch, 1978.

Young, John W., *Longman Guide to the Cold War and Détente 1941–91*, Longman, 1993.

Zagladin, Vadim, *The Soviet Peace Programme*, Novosti Press, 1984.

Zubok, Vladislav and Pleshakov, Constantine, *Inside the Kremlin's Cold War: From Stalin to Khrushchev*, Harvard University Press, 1996.

INDEX

Note: Page numbers in **bold** refer
to Background Narratives

SERENITY